D1539804

Diana

fashion & style

Beatrice Behlen & Joanna Marschner

*I soon developed a sense of how many different things the Princess had to be: a mother, a member of the royal family, the future Queen of England, an ambassador, an icon. She had all these roles to play, and, when asked, I as a designer was faced with the job of creating designs that would both reflect and enhance all of those roles … My dream from the beginning had been to deal with Diana as a **real person** – to me it was as important as the designing.*

Catherine Walker

Diana

fashion & style

Beatrice Behlen & Joanna Marschner

Jarrold Publishing in association with

**Historic Royal
PALACES**

Publication in this form copyright © Jarrold Publishing 2007.
Text copyright © Historic Royal Palaces 2007.
The moral right of the authors has been asserted.
Edited by Clare Murphy.
Designed by Green Tangerine.
Picture research by Jan Kean and Historic Royal Palaces.

The photographs are reproduced by kind permission of:
Alamy: 40 (Popperfoto), 49 (Bob Thomas); Camera Press London:
10 (PA/RBO), 16 (Lord Snowdon), 19 (Patrick Lichfield), 24l (Mariage
Charles DE GB), 24r (Diana Memorial Fund), 27 (Diana Memorial
Fund), 31 (Stewart Mark), 38 (Diana Memorial Fund), 53 (Diana
Memorial Fund), 58 (Diana Memorial Fund), 67 (Diana Memorial
Fund), 70 (Tony Drabble), 71 and 72 (Glen Harvey), 75 (Stewart
Mark), 78 (Diana Memorial Fund), 79 (Diana Memorial Fund), 80
(Richard Gillard), 83 (Lord Snowdon), 84 (Patrick Lichfield), 85 (Cecil
Beaton), 87 (Lord Snowdon), 88 (A.G. Karrick/Diana Memorial
Fund), 91 (Patrick Donovan), 92 (Lord Snowdon), 109 (Diana
Memorial Fund), 117 (Andrew Crowley); EMPICS: 12 (Andrew
Parsons); Historic Royal Palaces: front and back flaps, spine, 41,
42, 43, 50, 51, 56, 57, 76, 102, 103, 112, 113, 118, 119, 120,
121, 122, BC (all images © Stephen Hayward except 112); Rex
Features: FC (Tim Rooke), 15, 33 (Tim Rooke), 35, 36 (Steve
Wood), 37 (SIPA Press), 45 (Mauro Carraro), 47 (Mauro Carraro), 61
(Tim Rooke), 64 (Richard Young), 96 (Brendan Beirne), 98 (Today),
99, 101 (Dan Tuffs), 110; Mario Testino ©: 100; The Condé Nast
Publications Ltd: 95 (Patrick Demarchelier/Vogue); Tim Graham: 23,
28, 32, 54, 68, 77, 105, 108, 114, 125; TopFoto: 11, 14, 20 (by
Woodmansterne), 63; V & A Images: 106.

The dresses illustrated on pages 41, 42, 43, 56, 57, 76, 102, 103,
113, 118, 119, 120, 121 and 122 are on loan to Historic Royal
Palaces from Mrs Maureen Rorech Dunkel and The People's
Princess Charitable Foundation, Inc. The dress illustrated on pages
50 and 51 is on loan from Fontaine and Philip Minor, USA. The
dresses on these pages were photographed in the State
Apartments at Kensington Palace.

A CIP catalogue for this book is available from the British Library.

Produced under licence by Historic Royal Palaces Enterprises Limited.

Published by:
Jarrold Publishing
Healey House, Dene Road, Andover, Hampshire, SP10 2AA
www.jarrold-publishing.com

Set in Helvetica, Baskerville and Garamond.
Printed in China.

ISBN 978 1 84165 177 4   1/07

Historic Royal PALACES

Historic Royal Palaces is the
independent charity that looks
after the Tower of London,
Hampton Court Palace, the
Banqueting House, Kensington
Palace and Kew Palace. We help
everyone explore the story of
how monarchs and people have
shaped society, in some of the
greatest palaces ever built.

We receive no funding from the
Government or the Crown, so
we depend on the support of
our visitors, members, donors,
volunteers and sponsors.

Pitkin is an imprint of Jarrold Publishing, Norwich.

Contents

Foreword

By an accident of birth and timing and through her own infallible instinct, Diana, Princess of Wales had a unique position: the first member of any royal family to span the digital age and to understand the power of the instant image.

She seemed to sense from her arrival on the public stage in the early 1980s that the world of communication and of image-making was changing. She embraced the future and, in doing so, became part of that transformation. Acutely aware of the paparazzi lenses trained on her and clever enough to send out messages through her dresses and demeanour, Diana responded to the public glare by presenting a carefully-chosen reflection.

That is not to suggest that no previous royal had dressed for public consumption. From Elizabeth I in her jewelled bodices and rigid, face-framing ruffs to Queen Elizabeth The Queen Mother, dressed by Norman Hartnell and photographed by Cecil Beaton as a fairy-tale figure, former generations had been acutely aware of the language of clothes. Yet Hartnell's biography, *Silver and Gold*, showed how different attitudes were in an age of reverence when The Queen's 1953 coronation gown was not in any sense fashionable, but rather a costume heavy with symbolism.

For Diana, clothes were part of a charisma captured in the camera eye. But the process became increasingly thought-out and planned as the Princess took control of how she was represented.

You can trace the early moments of self-awareness when the 'shy Di' clothes – long skirts, country tweeds and sweaters or Cinderella ball gowns, all of which played a passive role in her appearance, became an active part of her royal persona. A major change came in 1983, when a one-shoulder dress by the Japanese designer Hachi outlined her figure and introduced an element of silver screen glamour. That was the start of a wardrobe as visual armour. Elements such as crystal beading, bold buttons or a surface sheen were specifically designed for the camera with the help of Victor Edelstein and Catherine Walker or the brash drama of Gianni Versace.

A decade later, when the world had found out that fairy tales can have a dark side (and when Diana had opted out of royal life), she put up for sale at auction many of her 1980s costumes. What made them significant was not the outfits themselves, but where and when they had been worn and the fact that the provenance had been diligently recorded.

In that same year – 1997 – the digital camera, developed since the beginning of the decade, became the ultimate paparazzi weapon. Any celebrity could now be captured, as Diana was, running to the gym, out with her children, on a hideaway holiday – on any occasion, public or private. And that image could be sent down the wires to cyberspace in the blink of one of her clear blue eyes.

How did the young Lady Diana Spencer morph into the glamorous Princess – and then take another path into the world of womanhood in her new life outside the royal family?

Royal figures – males as much as princesses and queens – have always required complicity from image makers, whether it was the portrait painters of the past or the photographers of today. The 20th-century visions of royalty developed with the art of photography and it was without doubt Cecil Beaton who created an image of awe without power in his sweetly romantic photographs.

Beaton's diaries traced his own royal trajectory from the hard-edged chic of the Duchess of Windsor in the wedding photographs of 1937 to the romantically regal portraits of the new Queen Elizabeth two years later. 'The queen looked a dream – a porcelain doll with flawless little face like luminous china', Beaton said of those 1939 post-abdication images. He had realized that it was the misty overall vision, rather than the specifics of hair, clothing or jewellery, that made the pictures iconic.

The photographer struggled to get the same effect with Princess Elizabeth, lamenting 'a certain heaviness that is not there in real life'. By the time of the 1953 coronation, the presence of live television and newsreel cameras for the first time created an emotional charge that impacted on Beaton's style of static portraiture. Significantly, the 'snapshots' of the post-1960s period seem the most vibrant and meaningful in documenting the changing royal image.

In Mario Testino, Diana found her Cecil Beaton – although in this case it was a photographer who stripped bare the trappings of royalty and let the Princess's natural character shine through. When you look at Diana's clothes today, they seem to define the 1980s rather than her persona. Yet her image is present in every fold of velvet or beaded bodice. That is why when dresses that had been accessories to major events in Diana's life were re-photographed by Testino, with her hair tousled and a little luminous make-up, he helped create her own language. The royal princess had morphed into an independent woman and the gowns became a chrysalis from which the real Diana emerged.

Suzy Menkes

Fashion Editor, International Herald Tribune

Diana, Princess of Wales

When Lady Diana Spencer married the Prince of Wales in St Paul's Cathedral in July 1981, she stepped into another world. She quickly became aware of the many new roles that she now had to fulfil. She was a member of the royal family – indeed the future queen – but she was also soon to become a mother of two small boys. She would be seen as an ambassador with a job to promote great and worthy causes. She would be held up as an example to others.

In the space of a few short years, Diana developed from a plump, pretty teenager to a sleek, groomed, international ambassador who used photography and photographers in the creation of her image. She brought a new approach to dressing for royal occasions and her outfits and even her hairstyles were widely copied – although Diana would be the first to give credit to her dress designers and milliners for her sartorial successes.

The social commentator Lord Blake stated: 'The real business of our monarchy is not mere glamour' and Diana certainly appreciated that there was a professional job to do. However, she knew instinctively that her beauty and a little glamour could be used to tremendous benefit in this. It would be through her dress that she established a continuous and tantalizing contact with the rest of the world, which surmounted any language barrier. Jasper Conran once caught the Princess standing in front of a rail of dresses debating 'what message will I be giving out if I wear this?'. Her intuition served her well and despite her lack of

Diana Frances Spencer, aged 2. Her dress with its smocked bodice and her sensible shoes with an instep strap are typical wear for a well-dressed child in the 1960s.

This photograph of Lady Diana Spencer, taken by Lord Snowdon, was published in Vogue *in February 1981, shortly before her engagement to the Prince of Wales was announced. Diana wears a pale-pink chiffon blouse by David and Elizabeth Emanuel.*

Althorp House in Northamptonshire, the
ancestral home of the Spencer family.
There has been a house on this site since
the beginning of the 16th century. In the
late 18th century the house was remodelled
for George John, 2nd Earl Spencer by the
distinguished architect, Henry Holland.

academic credentials, Diana became one of the most
effective communicators of the 20th century.

The Honourable Diana Frances Spencer was born on 1 July
1961 at Park House on the Sandringham Estate in Norfolk.
She was the third daughter of Edward John, Viscount
Althorp and his wife Frances. As a young man Viscount
Althorp had served as equerry to King George VI between
1950 and 1952. Frances was the daughter of Ruth, Lady
Fermoy, a lady-in-waiting to the late Queen Mother and was
one of her closest friends. This tradition of close personal
service to the royal family ensured that Diana, together with
her two elder sisters, Sarah and Jane, and their little brother,
Charles, grew up playing with the younger royal children,
Prince Andrew and Prince Edward, when they visited
Sandringham House nearby.

All looked set for an idyllic childhood. Park House was
spacious and set in lovely gardens with plenty of space
for games. However, when Diana was just 7 years old
her parents separated and later divorced. Custody of the
children was awarded to Viscount Althorp and the pattern
of their lives would change dramatically.

Diana received her early education at home and later
attended a small day school in King's Lynn. At the age

of 9 she was sent to boarding school at Riddlesworth Hall in Norfolk. Her sunny nature meant she quickly made many friends there. The school allowed pupils to bring in their small pets from home. Diana was accompanied by her guinea pig, Peanut, and took great pleasure in helping out in the 'Pets' Corner'.

In 1973 Diana joined West Heath School near Sevenoaks in Kent. While she did not excel at academic subjects, she greatly enjoyed dancing and swimming. West Heath had an imaginative programme of community service. Pupils were provided with opportunities to assist older citizens and to participate in activities in local hospitals. Muriel Simmons, who worked for Sevenoaks Voluntary Services and acted as an intermediary with the school, recalls how Diana, even at a young age, was not intimidated by any encounter and would find imaginative ways of engaging with the patients. She even found a way of dancing while pushing a wheelchair.

The suit Diana wore on the day her engagement to Prince Charles was announced was bought 'off the peg' at Harrods. It was bright blue, matching the colour of her striking sapphire engagement ring.

Diana with some of her young charges at the Young England Kindergarten in 1980. She unwittingly stood with her back to the sun and her flimsy skirt appeared see-through.

When Diana was 13, her grandfather died, and her father became the 8th Earl Spencer. The Honourable Diana was now Lady Diana Spencer. Home was Althorp House in Northamptonshire, an estate bought by a John Spencer who had died in 1522 and who had made his fortune in sheep farming. In 1976 Diana's father remarried. His second wife was Raine, daughter of Barbara Cartland. Diana's mother had already remarried and had moved to Scotland with her new husband, Peter Shand Kydd.

Unsettled by arrangements at home and being prevented by homesickness from completing a year at the Institut Alpin Videmanette, a finishing school in Switzerland, Diana decided to follow her older sisters to London. She moved into a flat in Earls Court and took a series of part-time jobs as a nanny and cleaner for friends and acquaintances.

Diana's sister Jane had been at school with Kay King who ran the Young England Kindergarten in Pimlico. In 1979 Jane asked her friend if there might be an opening there for her sister. Although she was by far the youngest of the team of assistants, Diana's empathy with small children was soon apparent and she was employed for nearly two years.

It was during a visit to Althorp in 1977 that Diana encountered Prince Charles for the first time since her childhood. The Prince was attending a shooting party and Diana recorded afterwards she had found him 'pretty amazing'. It was not long before Charles, 12 years her senior, truly began to take an interest in the unaffected, fresh-faced young Diana. When the Prince sent an invitation to Diana's sister Jane and her new husband, Robert Fellowes, to attend his 30th birthday party in 1978, he suggested that Diana might like to come along too.

A romance soon developed, and on 8 September 1980 *The Sun* printed the headline 'He's in love again. Lady Di is the new girl for Charles'. The following week the *Daily Mail* printed a photograph of Diana and asked 'Has Charles

This photograph by Lord Snowdon was published following the announcement of the engagement between Diana and Prince Charles. Diana wears a green silk taffeta dress by Nettie Vogues.

found his girl?'. The engagement between the Prince of
Wales and Lady Diana Spencer was announced on
24 February 1981, and Diana encountered her first sartorial
challenge. As she was quick to point out, at this time she
possessed one long dress, one silk blouse and one pair of
smart shoes to go with her £30,000 diamond and sapphire
engagement ring. Her mother suggested that a visit to her
favourite dressmaker, Bellville Sassoon, might be in order to
obtain a suitable outfit for all the inevitable press calls.
However, Diana, a devotee of Laura Ashley, Miss Selfridge
and Peter Jones, was so unfamiliar with the world of the
couturier that she lost her courage before any purchase was
made. A rather conservative 'off the peg' sapphire blue suit
by Cojana was hastily purchased at Harrods. Diana wore it
with a silk shirt with a large floppy bow tied at the neck.

Months of speculation about the design of Diana's wedding
dress ended on 29 July 1981. 'The romantic ruffle that the
Princess has made her trademark was the whole point of
her fairy-tale wedding dress', remarked the fashion journalist
Suzy Menkes. For this important commission Diana turned to
David and Elizabeth Emanuel. She had encountered their
work during a photo shoot organized by Lord Snowdon for
Vogue in 1981 when she had admired their pale-pink chiffon
blouse and taffeta skirt. The Emanuels designed for her a
wedding dress in ivory silk taffeta with a close-fitting bodice
overlaid at the centre front and back with panels of antique
Carrickmacross lace from Queen Mary's collection. The
gently scooped neckline and the large puffed sleeves were

*Diana bends down to speak to
her youngest bridesmaid, 5-year-
old Clementine Hambro, on their
way out to the balcony at
Buckingham Palace to greet
the crowds of well-wishers.
The Queen, wearing a dress of
turquoise crêpe with a flower-
trimmed hat, looks on.*

Diana arrives at St Paul's Cathedral on her wedding day. India Hicks, aged 13, one of her bridesmaids, later remarked: 'I have seen crowds and listened to applause, but I have never heard anything like that noise when Diana got out of the carriage. It was absolutely extraordinary – the cheers and cries of the people. Then Sarah [Lady Sarah Armstrong-Jones] and I kind of went to work on straightening out that train.'

trimmed with bows and deep ruffles of taffeta and embroidered lace. The skirt was very full and was supported on a mountain of stiff net petticoats. The train extending 25 feet behind the bride fastened on at the waist. As had become traditional when making a royal wedding dress, the designers had sought out material of British origin. Some of the silk was spun from silk worms raised at Lullingstone Castle in Dorset. Lace trimmings used in addition to the antique lace were manufactured by Roger Watson, lacemakers in Nottingham. Diana chose to wear the Spencer family tiara with her veil made of silk tulle supplied by John Heathcoat in Devon, which was studded with hundreds of mother of pearl sequins. She borrowed a pair of striking diamond earrings from her mother.

The dress was made by a single seamstress, Nina Missetzis, in a locked room on the fourth floor of the Emanuel's studio. She sewed a tiny blue bow into the waistband so that in the age-old tradition Diana would be wearing something blue as well as her new dress trimmed with antique lace and her mother's borrowed earrings. There was also a little 18-carat Welsh-gold horseshoe stitched into the back of the dress for extra luck. Mrs Missetzis recalled that Lady Diana shivered when she tried on the dress: 'There were tears in her eyes. She kissed me and said: "Thank you, Nina, thank you".'

Diana's wedding shoes were made by Clive Shilton. They were low-heeled silk satin-covered pumps, embroidered in

Lady Diana shivered when she tried on the dress: 'There were tears in her eyes. She kissed me and said: "Thank you, Nina, thank you".'

Seamstress Nina Missetzis

a trellis pattern, decorated with mother of pearl sequins. Applied over each toe was a lace-trimmed and beaded heart-shaped rosette. Mr Shilton was careful to paint the soles of the shoes with a design of stylized flowers and the letters C and D entwined just in case anyone should catch a glimpse of them as the bride knelt down.

To complete the ensemble, the Emanuels supplied a lace-trimmed purse to hold a handkerchief and an ivory taffeta umbrella to tuck into the carriage in case the weather should break on the way home.

Hundreds of thousands of people flocked to London to line the streets between Buckingham Palace and St Paul's Cathedral on the day of the wedding. Over 750 million others turned on their televisions to follow the celebrations. There was a universal gasp at the first sight of Diana as she rode with her father in the glass coach to St Paul's. Nick Scoging, in charge of production at Welsh Bride Ltd in Cardigan, sitting poised with his team to turn out instant copies of the dress, exclaimed 'Christ, the dress fills the whole coach!'. 'Gosh – look at the train – it's huge!' added June Vernon, the machinist.

It took Lady Sarah Armstrong-Jones and India Hicks, Diana's teenage bridesmaids, some minutes to organize the

Diana and Charles leave St Paul's Cathedral after the wedding service, Diana's train streaming behind her. David Emanuel recalled designing the dress: 'At the time she was absolutely ecstatic ... She was a bride. She was so excited! What she was saying was "Oh do you think the train is big enough? What's the biggest train? Oh, we are going to make it bigger" – and then having made it bigger, "Do you think it should be bigger?" It was a joke. It was magic'.

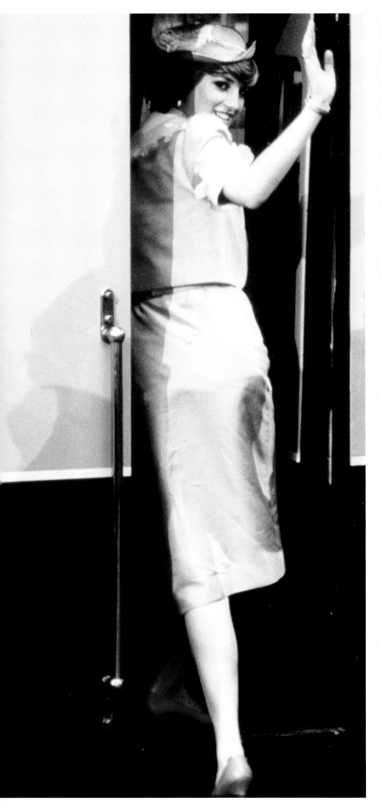

Diana's 'going away' outfit was made by Bellville Sassoon. Diana ordered two jackets, one with long sleeves, and the other with short. She chose to wear the short-sleeved version as she left Waterloo station for her honeymoon. The long-sleeved jacket was later worn during a visit to Australia in 1983.

billowing mass of train behind her as she made her way up the steps to the cathedral. There they rejoined their companion attendants to accompany the bride up the aisle. Lady Sarah, the eldest, wore a full-length dress of ivory taffeta with a ruffled neckline, large lace-trimmed puffed sleeves and a lace-trimmed overskirt. There was an old-gold sash at her waist tied in a big bow behind. The dresses worn by India and the three little girls, Sarah-Jane Gaselee, Catherine Cameron and Clementine Hambro, were of the same style, but ballerina length. The hair of all the girls was dressed with garlands of meadow flowers and ivy, which also tumbled from the small baskets they carried. There were two young pages, Lord Nicholas Windsor and Edward van Cutsem, dressed in replicas of the naval cadets' uniforms worn when another Prince of Wales, Albert Edward, the eldest son of Queen Victoria, married Princess Alexandra of Denmark in 1863.

Diana carried a large trailing bouquet made up by the florist Longmans. It was composed of gold Mountbatten roses, white freesias, lily of the valley, stephanotis, white odontoglossum orchids and long flowing sprays of ivy. Tucked into the mix were tiny sprays of myrtle and veronica, which have traditionally been carried by all royal brides since Queen Victoria's wedding in 1840.

The next day, the wedding dress was widely praised in the British press: the *Daily Mail* called Diana 'the most breathtaking bride in history' and Jackie Modlinger from the

'Diana was an intuitive dresser; she did not primarily dress for the fashion intelligentsia. As the most photographed woman in history, she was dressing for a very wide audience, and in doing so she touched many hearts.'

Catherine Walker

Daily Express thought the 'dress fitted and looked like a dream'. No article was complete without the adjective 'fairy tale'. There were a few dissenting voices: some found the sleeves too bouffant and the material ill-chosen as it creased. However, the dress was dramatic and wildly romantic and within the vast lofty interior of St Paul's Cathedral was more than able to hold its own. The overall effect was stunning. From beginning to end every observer had to admit it was truly a day to remember.

Diana left for her honeymoon, with her prince, wearing a pretty coral-coloured dress by Bellville Sassoon trimmed round the neckline with ruffles that spilled over the short-sleeved matching bolero. John Boyd provided the small jaunty hat covered with the same fabric and topped with a flourish of ostrich feathers. The Princess was learning: being astute and practical she asked the designers also to supply a long-sleeved version of the jacket which she could wear if the weather turned. The honeymoon was spent at Broadlands in Hampshire, before the couple took a cruise on the royal yacht *Britannia* and finished with a holiday at Balmoral Castle in Scotland.

In March 1981 Prince Charles's Assistant Private Secretary, Oliver Everett, was assigned to look after the

Diana wore a figure-hugging dress of crushed velvet by Catherine Walker for the film premiere of Back to the Future *in 1985. One of the dress's most dramatic design features was a very low-cut back, which the Princess drew attention to by wearing a long string of pearls knotted behind.*

Diana, in a smart but practical suit, talks to a young girl after opening the National Institute of Conductive Education at Cannon Hill House, Moseley, Birmingham in 1995.

Princess's interests. As numerous charities approached the Princess he gathered together all their requests for patronage. Together they agreed that the Princess would concentrate on promoting causes close to her heart at that time – children, charities dealing with Welsh concerns, and music and ballet – a passion since childhood. The Princess eventually became the patron of over a hundred charities and would discover that a substantial wardrobe of smart daywear would be required for the many visits she would make and lunches she would attend. In the evening there would be an enormous number of glittering functions where spectacular dresses and ball gowns were needed.

From her first royal tour of the principality of Wales in November 1981, the Princess was swept off by Prince Charles into a lively programme of visits around the world. There was, of course, time for fun and relaxation, such as watching Prince Charles playing polo, or tramping over the moors in Scotland, but even on these occasions Diana learnt that a crowd could quickly gather and photographers appear. She could enjoy few unguarded moments.

The Princess soon had other important preoccupations. Less than a year after their wedding, on 21 June 1982, the couple celebrated the birth of their first child, Prince William Arthur Philip Louis. On 15 September 1984, their second son, Prince Henry Charles Albert David, was born. He has always been known as Prince Harry. The Prince and Princess delighted in the two young boys and insisted that

Prince William should accompany them on their tour of Australia in 1983 when he was just a few months old.

Diana's proven ability in dealing sensitively and imaginatively with children, and her experience in establishing a rapport and empathy with the ill or elderly, developed dramatically. She was never fearful of promoting what were seen as being 'difficult' causes, such as leprosy and AIDS, or politically sensitive issues such as landmines. After a visit to Nigeria in 1990 where Diana met people who had been crippled by leprosy, she became patron of the Leprosy Mission. The following year she was made patron of the National AIDS Trust.

In 1992, to the great distress of the Princess, it became impossible to disguise the fact that her marriage to the Prince of Wales had broken down. In June, Andrew Morton published his revealing biography in which her unhappiness was disclosed. When the royal couple visited South Korea later in the year their estrangement was clear to the whole world and in December John Major, the Prime Minister, finally announced that the couple had decided to separate.

The Princess realized that her effectiveness at promoting the work of many of her charities would be compromised by her change in status and she resigned from over a hundred of them. However, there were six concerns where she felt she could still have a role to play. These were Centrepoint – a charity for the homeless – the National AIDS Trust, the Leprosy Mission, the English National Ballet, Great Ormond Street Hospital for Sick Children and the Royal Marsden Hospital specializing in cancer research and treatment. For these charities the Princess continued to work energetically.

With the broadcasting of Diana's controversial interview with Martin Bashir on 20 November 1995, watched by over 20 million viewers, and Prince Charles's with Jonathan Dimbleby on 24 June the previous year, which reached a similar audience, it was absolutely clear that there would be no chance of a reconciliation between the couple. Their decree nisi was granted by the court on 15 July 1996, followed by the decree absolute on 28 August.

Sad as she was that her marriage had foundered, just like that of her parents, Diana now had confidence and energy and was determined to look at the future positively. For Diana, who lost her title, Her Royal Highness, and became just Diana, Princess of Wales, this was the start of a new life. It is revealing that on the evening when Prince Charles's interview was broadcast,

Diana arrives at a party at the Serpentine Gallery on the evening Jonathan Dimbleby's interview with Prince Charles was broadcast to the nation in 1994. She wears a bold cocktail dress by Athens-trained Christina Stambolian, and high heels.

On 21 July 1997, Diana attended her last official engagement visiting the children's unit of Northwick Park and St Mark's Hospital in north-west London. She wore a bright-red dress by Catherine Walker, with minimal gold trimmings. It was simple and understated.

In 1997, Diana became involved in the campaign against landmines in a practical way. She visited Angola under the auspices of the Red Cross and, wearing body armour and face protection, walked through the minefields before visiting those who had been injured.

the Princess was invited to a reception at the Serpentine Gallery in London. She chose to wear a dress by Christina Stambolian. It was short and tightly fitting, made of pleated black silk, with a delicate black silk chiffon streamer floating from one hip. She wore high heels, black stockings and a spectacular pearl and sapphire necklace with her engagement ring. It was the ultimate stylish and sexy outfit, carried off to perfection.

Interestingly, the last images of Diana that most people will be able to call to mind are those of her wearing chinos, a simple cotton shirt, low-heeled moccasins and body armour as she walked through the minefields of Angola in January 1997. She was tanned and fit with her hair sharply cut. Diana had become such a powerful communicator that she no longer needed elaborate dresses to ensure that the camera lenses of the world would follow her every step. She had the confidence to know that her strength of character would shine through whatever she wore. Lovely dresses were of course a great delight on the right occasions, but she no longer needed them as an emotional prop.

In September 1996, the Princess decided to auction 79 of her dresses at Christie's in New York. She credited Prince William with having the idea that this could raise money for her favourite charities. The sale, held on 25 June 1997, raised over three million dollars. While it has been suggested that some of the dresses were very dear favourites and that the Princess was sad to see them go, it also marked

'She was the most perfect example of a young beautiful and modern woman with her very own style. No fashion victim, but a personality 100 per cent of today.'

Karl Lagerfeld

another watershed: from a practical and emotional point of view this part of her wardrobe had become redundant. Meredith Etherington-Smith, then Creative and Marketing Director at Christie's, who worked with Diana on the selection of the dresses, recalled the Princess confiding: 'My life, as you know, has changed and these are all part of my old life. So why shouldn't someone else benefit from them? I can't exactly send them to a charity shop: someone would be bound to recognize them.'

Maureen Rorech Dunkel from Florida purchased 14 dresses at the sale including the dramatic dark blue velvet dress made by Victor Edelstein in which the Princess had danced with John Travolta at the White House in 1985 (see page 110). In 1999 Mrs Rorech Dunkel loaned these dresses to Kensington Palace, where they were placed on public display. In 2005 she added another dress: an elegant, white, lace-trimmed dress by Bruce Oldfield (page 42). The collection at Kensington also includes a white organdy dress embroidered with gold by David and Elizabeth Emanuel, loaned by Fontaine and Philip Minor (see page 50).

Diana, Princess of Wales was tragically killed in a car crash in Paris on 31 August 1997 aged just 36. Her funeral took place at Westminster Abbey on 6 September. She is buried at her family home, Althorp in Northamptonshire.

Diana's funeral was held at Westminster Abbey on 6 September 1997. Prince Charles and her two young sons, Prince William and Prince Harry, together with her brother, Lord Spencer, and the Duke of Edinburgh walked behind the coffin.

The development of the Princess's style

When the 19-year-old Lady Diana Spencer became engaged to the Prince of Wales in February 1981, she had to adapt her dress style to her new status and role. The day before the engagement was officially announced, Diana moved to Clarence House, the London residence of The Queen Mother, before taking up a suite of rooms in Buckingham Palace. Here, together with her mother and a small team of helpers, she made preparations for her wedding and new wardrobe.

Photographs of the teenage Diana show her in clothes that many women of a similar age would have worn in the 1970s: flowery Laura Ashley (real or inspired) or 'ethnic' dresses, tight jeans with big sweaters or blouses over roll-necks, dungarees and the staples of the landed gentry: wellies and quilted Huskie jackets and waistcoats. In the autumn of 1980, the Press got wind of the royal romance and started to follow Diana on her way to and from work. She was photographed by the paparazzi in blouses with pie-crust collars under cardigans or V-neck sweaters worn with tight-fitting corduroy trousers or gathered skirts. Her favourite accessories were patterned cotton neckerchiefs, a pearl necklace or silver locket and flat shoes.

This was the wardrobe of the typical 'Sloane Ranger', a term coined by the social commentator Peter York in 1975 for young upper-middle class women living not too far from Sloane Square in west London. The original Sloane Ranger look, which had included the ubiquitous pearls, Gucci

Diana photographed in 1980 in the outfit of a typical Sloane Ranger. A personal touch is provided by the large man's watch that Diana even wore with her engagement suit.

Princess Anne did not shy away from fashionable clothes and wore mini skirts and trouser suits in the 1960s and 1970s. This photograph was taken during a visit to Ecuador in 1973.

In the early 1980s, Diana favoured pretty suits for formal occasions. They were often made of velvet and worn with pie-crust collar or pussy-bow blouses and neat hats. For the Guards Chapel Remembrance Day service in November 1983, Diana wore a green suit by Caroline Charles with a matching hat by John Boyd.

When Diana and her mother returned to *Vogue* for fashion advice, Felicity Clark and the editor-in-chief, Beatrice Miller, suggested the fashion editor, Anna Harvey, to assist Diana. Harvey assembled clothes for Diana to choose from, either at the *Vogue* headquarters in central London, or later at Kensington Palace.

loafers, a quilted Chanel bag and a Hermès scarf knotted under the chin, had changed by the time Peter York and Ann Barr published their *Official Sloane Ranger Handbook* in 1985. In it, Diana is described as 'a walking lesson in Mark II Sloane style at its best'; she is the 'Supersloane'.

The Sloane style was one of the many 'niche' fashions that emerged during the 1970s. The breaking down of traditional class and gender divisions during the previous two decades was reflected in fashion. Until now high fashion had been generated by the great couture houses in France, and to a lesser extent in England and Italy. It was first worn by a wealthy elite before trickling down the social scale. The increasing importance of youth culture and the emergence of subcultures meant that now new fashions were 'bubbling up'

from below. Ethnic and retro-inspired mainstream fashion sat side by side with subcultural styles such as the hippie look and punk, black style, glam rock and disco. Some of the styles spawned by the subcultures made their way on to the High Street, but they were not an option for Diana.

It was not easy to determine what kind of wardrobe was appropriate for a 1980s teenage Princess who would soon be the most senior royal woman after The Queen and The Queen Mother. Royal dress, not just in Britain but worldwide, was traditionally more formal than mainstream fashion and this difference became more prominent during the course of the 20th century. When Queen Elizabeth II, then still a Princess, had assumed her public role in the 1940s, she had worn formal suits with a hat and gloves on official engagements, at the time the standard

Diana at Smith's Lawn, the grounds of the Guards Polo Club in Windsor, in May 1982, one month before the birth of Prince William. She is wearing a green silk crêpe de Chine smock dress by Catherine Walker and carrying her favourite Souleiado bag.

This 1930s-style evening dress in dark green silk velvet by Victor Edelstein is unusually restrained for 1985 when Diana still favoured elaborate and frilly evening gowns.

uniform of a well-to-do young lady. While suits made a comeback in the 1980s, even Sloane Rangers reserved hats and gloves only for special occasions.

There were no recent royal role models Diana could follow. Princess Anne, who had started to undertake royal and official duties at the same age as Diana, had followed contemporary fashion to some extent: she wore mini skirts and sometimes even fashionable trouser suits. But that had been more than ten years ago. Adopting the more casual style of European royals was out of the question. Princess Caroline of Monaco, only four years older than Diana, wore ultra-fashionable clothes and in 1977 had even posed for a semi-official family photograph in a stars-and-stripes swimsuit, something that would have been deemed highly inappropriate in Britain.

Diana's mother and her sisters, Jane and Sarah, played a prominent part in creating Diana's early style. Both sisters had worked for *Vogue* before they were married and had remained friends with the beauty editor, Felicity Clark. Clark had been instrumental in the commissioning and publishing of the first of the many images of Diana that were to appear in the magazine. Diana had been picked as one of the debutantes to be included in *Vogue's* regular spring feature. By chance the photographs, taken by Lord Snowdon, Prince Charles's uncle, appeared in the February issue and thus coincided with the announcement of the royal engagement.

When Diana and her mother returned to *Vogue* for fashion advice, Felicity Clark and the editor-in-chief, Beatrice Miller, suggested the fashion editor, Anna Harvey, to assist Diana. Harvey assembled clothes for Diana to choose from, either at the *Vogue* headquarters in central London, or later at Kensington Palace. The *Sunday People*'s royal correspondent, Jane Owen, noted in 1983 that 'by and large the designs Anna Harvey chooses for the "Royal Rail" are from off-the-peg warehouse designers, such as Jan Vanvelden, Bill Pashley, David Neill, Gina Fratini'. Bill Pashley had been patronized by Diana's mother, who also introduced her daughter to other top London designers such as Jean Muir, Belinda Bellville and David Sassoon, and the hat maker

Some of the unwritten rules governing royal dress were contradictory: the Princess was expected not to wear the same clothes too often while at the same time avoiding accusations of spending too much money on her appearance.

The influence of Diana's early romantic style is still clearly visible in this off-white satin dress with frilly lace blouse by Bruce Oldfield from 1990. The wide shoulders are a remnant from the 1980s power look that the Princess was fond of. The dress was worn at a private view in 1990 and at a banquet at Buckingham Palace the following year.

John Boyd. Her sister Jane introduced Diana to Donald Campbell and, having bought one or two of her designs in the past, Diana was already familiar with the work of Caroline Charles, who provided dresses for the Duchess of Kent and Princess Margaret. Like other members of the royal family, Diana was expected to support British fashion, rather than buying from designers abroad.

Many of these designers would have been aware of the restrictions imposed when creating dress for members of the royal family. Clothes have to be practical and perform well in difficult situations, as Diana explained in 1985: 'You'd be amazed what one has to worry about, from the obvious things like the wind – because there's always a gale wherever we go – and the wind is my enemy, there's no doubt about that. And you've got to put your arm up to get some flowers, so you can't have something too revealing, and you can't have hems too short because when you bend over there's six children looking up your skirt'.

Caroline Charles recalled: 'We used to rehearse necklines, making sure they weren't too low, thinking about how she'd have to decorously get out of a car and face the waiting photographers'. This lesson was learnt the hard way at Diana's first official engagement, a charity banquet held on 10 March 1981 at Goldsmiths' Hall in London. Diana wore a black silk taffeta, off-the-shoulder ball gown purchased off-the-peg from David and Elizabeth Emanuel. There was no time to make any alterations to the dress and when Diana got out of the car that evening, the revealing bodice proved to be a problem, a fact that was readily exploited by the media the next day: the *Daily Express* called it 'Di's Daring Debut' while the *Daily Mirror*'s headline ran:

'Lady Di takes the plunge'. Diana made sure not to make this mistake again and often covered her décolletage with her hands or her handbag when getting out of cars.

As The Queen Mother before her, The Queen often wears bright colours to make her stand out in a crowd, but Diana's 5 feet 10 inches made this less important. Royal clothes also have to photograph well, a lesson Diana learnt very early on. In September 1980, Diana posed for a series of photographs in the garden of the Young England Kindergarten. Surrounded by her charges, she was photographed with the sun behind her, revealing the silhouette of her long legs underneath her flimsy, patterned skirt. Diana explained: 'I was so nervous about the whole thing, I never thought I would be standing with the light behind me'. Even though she would later laugh about the incident, she learnt quickly, and the mistake was never repeated.

Some of the unwritten rules governing royal dress were contradictory: the Princess was expected not to wear the same clothes too often while at the same time avoiding accusations of spending too much money on her appearance. In 1985 Diana recalled the preparations for the couple's first tour abroad: 'I had to buy endless new things, of course, because on a tour you change three or four times

Extremely wide, padded shoulders and bouffant hair epitomized 1980s power dressing. Diana wore this bright-red dress by Victor Edelstein during a tour of Australia in 1985. In her 'Dynasty Di' phase, Diana favoured metallic accessories.

a day'. This spending spree incited comments: 'The arrival of all the new things was causing tremendous criticism, but what else could I do? I couldn't go around in a leopard skin'. Not every outfit worn abroad was new; Diana often recycled her favourite dresses and suits or had them slightly altered. But when Diana reused dresses during a visit to Italy in March 1985, the Press complained again. The Princess was not going to change her approach: 'Well, I'm afraid you're going to see everything time and time again because it fits, it's comfortable, and it still works. You know, I feel that a lot of people thought I was going on a fashion tour for two weeks. I wasn't. I was going along to support the British flag, with my husband, as his wife'.

Diana's clothes also had to make at least a nod to fashion while never giving the impression that she was obsessed with the latest looks. At first, this long catalogue of demands was not entirely clear to Diana and her advisors, but her clothes developed in consideration of them and from the start were ruthlessly commented upon.

Diana soon established a style of dressing which she followed until the mid-1980s. On official day visits in colder months she wore suits, usually composed of tight-fitting jackets and straight or pleated skirts with pussy-bow or pie-crust collar blouses. Like The Queen, the Princess could wear almost any colour and her palette ranged from beige over bright pink and blues to dark purple and, very rarely, black. During the summer the suits were exchanged for

In the early 1980s, Diana often wore clothing that seemed to have been made for someone much older. This powder-pink, candy-striped dress and short jacket by Catherine Walker is an example of this and of 'royal recycling'. It was worn in Australia and Canada in 1983 and again in Italy in 1985.

'For Scotland it was tartan, for the country, if it were, say, a visit to a hospice, we would design a more friendly or colourful and informal suit. For London it would be something sharper for the day, and for the evening there was the demanding task of designing something that was not extravagant like you would do for a catwalk show, but something that matched her multifaceted stature as a beautiful princess, young mother, and future Queen.'

Catherine Walker

patterned silk or cotton dresses, often with large white collars, worn with shoes in matching colours. In June 1981, at her first Royal Ascot, Diana had worn white gloves, but this was a traditional royal custom that she soon abandoned, despite the fact that Anna Harvey had ordered dozens and dozens of suede gloves in every shade. Harvey explained that Diana 'wanted flesh to flesh contact. Hats, on the other hand, were something she didn't feel able to dispense with for years'.

This general pattern was only slightly disturbed during the Princess's pregnancies. Diana started to wear loose-fitting dresses and coats soon after her first pregnancy was officially announced in November 1981. High-waisted dresses of light silk or cotton fabrics with small patterns were ordered, amongst others, from Jasper Conran, Caroline Charles, Bellville Sassoon, David Neill and from the Chelsea Design Company, Catherine Walker's

couture business. Until the spring, these dresses remained hidden under a number of brightly-coloured woollen coats by Bellville Sassoon. During her second pregnancy, announced in February 1984, the Princess waited longer before adopting maternity wear. While she continued to wear traditional maternity dresses, particularly those made by Jan Vanvelden, distinguished by their large collars, she also wore a number of drop-waisted dresses. One of those, an ice-blue silk satin dress by Catherine Walker, was credited by the *Evening Standard* as forever having changed 'the silhouette of maternity clothes'.

Diana tried to incorporate into her outfits the traditional colours or fabrics associated with the places she visited. On her first tour of Wales, soon after the wedding, Diana delighted the many onlookers by wearing a Donald Campbell suit in red and green, the Welsh national colours. In Scotland,

The royal family often wear tartan in Scotland. For the Highland Gathering at Braemar in 1982 Diana chose a dress by Caroline Charles, and a Glengarry, the traditional cap of Scottish regiments.

This embroidered silk satin and organza dress is a perfect example of David and Elizabeth Emanuel's romantic style. The dress was not made especially for the Princess, but bought at a charity auction for the Red Cross. Diana wore it on three occasions during 1986 and 1987.

the royal family often dresses in traditional Scottish tartan, or country tweeds. When Diana visited the Braemar Gathering, the annual Highland Games, in 1981, she wore a tartan suit by Caroline Charles and a tam-o'-shanter, a type of bonnet worn by the Scottish infantry regiments of the British Army. Catherine Walker, one of the Princess's favourite designers, explained:

> For Scotland it was tartan, for the country, if it were, say, a visit to a hospice, we would design a more friendly or colourful and informal suit. For London it would be something sharper for the day, and for the evening there was the demanding task of designing something that was not extravagant like you would do for a catwalk show, but something that matched her multifaceted stature as a beautiful princess, young mother, and future Queen.

When the royal couple visited the Middle East in 1985, the Princess's wardrobe had to meet a different set of requirements. The photographer Jayne Fincher remembered that female journalists were advised to cover their arms and to keep garments loose-fitting. When The Queen had visited Saudi Arabia in 1976 she had worn full-length gowns even for daytime functions, but Diana chose calf-length skirts and dresses. The finale of the visit

'In the early eighties Diana's designs had to be more elaborate, had to look special in a particular way, and all the little details – the buttons, the binding – helped to reflect this. It felt as though Diana needed a sort of royal uniform that was a legacy from eighteenth-century English court dressing, where etiquette decreed that sartorial finery and rich apparel were appropriate.'

Catherine Walker

was a desert picnic, a two-hour drive from the capital Riyadh. Diana knew she would be expected to sit on carpets and instead of a dress wore white trousers and a loose, long sleeved tunic by Catherine Walker.

The Princess's official clothes in the early 1980s were not what a young woman in her early twenties would have been expected to wear. Many of Diana's outfits seemed to have been made for someone much older than herself. For John Boyd, Diana was 'a poor wee lassie dressing up in her mother's clothes'. Catherine Walker commented:

In the early eighties Diana's designs had to be more elaborate, had to look special in a particular way, and all the little details – the buttons, the binding – helped to reflect this. It felt as though Diana needed a sort of royal uniform that was a legacy from eighteenth-century English court dressing, where etiquette decreed that sartorial finery and rich apparel were appropriate.

In November 1982, not long after the birth of Prince William, Diana attended a fashion show in a dress by Bruce Oldfield that accentuated her painfully thin arms. She was suffering

During a state visit to America in 1985, Diana wore many wide-shouldered power suits. By coincidence or design, Catherine Walker's black and white suit and Frederick Fox's hat were a perfect match for the background at the National Gallery, Washington DC.

from post-natal depression and bulimia, but allowed none of her private battles to interfere with her public duties. Diana's obvious weight loss received a lot of media attention, not all of it negative. Some writers, apparently agreeing with the Duchess of Windsor that a woman can never be too thin, applauded the Princess's new, slim figure and it seems that it also prompted Diana to adopt some sleeker styles, particularly for her evening wear.

When the royal couple undertook their first tour of Australia and New Zealand in 1983, Diana caused a sensation by wearing a slim-line dress by the London-based Japanese designer Hachi. The heavily beaded, one-sleeved dress of cream chiffon foreshadowed the less frilly styles Diana was soon to adopt. Not everybody liked this new style. Anna Harvey, who had selected the dress, remembered that 'the establishment hated it. It was too revealing; they didn't think it was Royal. After that she was dubbed Dynasty Di and rarely wore full skirts'. Diana was a big fan of *Dynasty* and never missed an episode of this popular American soap. While she probably did not consciously model herself after the female leads, she admitted in 1985: 'Sometimes I can be a little outrageous, which is quite nice. Sometimes'. Diana was not alone in her love of flamboyant styles, shiny fabrics and bright colours. The fashions depicted in the television series found their way, in modified form, on to the High Street and many women could be seen in big jackets with padded shoulders, tight skirts and high heels, with carefully highlighted and layered hair.

Diana at a gala dinner in Washington in 1985. The figure-hugging beaded dress by the Japanese-born designer Hachi caused a sensation when Diana first wore it in Australia two years earlier. It marked her departure from the early 'fairy-princess' style towards a more streamlined look.

Diana's late 1980s wardrobe was also influenced by two other, related popular styles. In the early part of the decade, the Italian designers Armani and Cerutti led the way in producing a version of what became know as 'power dressing': Marlene Dietrich trousers or slim skirts worn with straight-cut jackets. In 1977 the American author John Molloy had advocated an ultra-cautious, conservative uniform in *The Woman's Dress for Success Book* for female executives who wanted to make their way in a still largely male-dominated working environment. Molloy prescribed calf-length skirts and masculine jackets, their severity softened by feminine touches such as silk blouses, soft bow ties, earrings and manicured nails. During the royal couple's visit to the United States in 1985 Diana was seen in many such 'power suits' and they remained her official daywear until the end of the decade.

Looking at photographs of Diana from the time of her engagement to the separation in 1992, it is hard to pin down exactly what the Diana look was. There were signature styles: the immaculate hair, the earrings (either real or costume jewellery), the court shoes in a variety of colours (although black patent leather seemed to have been a favourite), and the large variety of clutch bags in colours matching her outfits. Until the late 1980s, Diana obtained her official wardrobe from a large number of designers and her style seemed to change according to whose clothes she was wearing. This was particularly apparent in her evening wardrobe. In the first half of the 1980s Diana preferred

The timelessness of some of Catherine Walker's designs for Diana is exemplified by this light grey dress with bow detail and beaded bodice. Made in 1990, the dress was worn at private occasions and for Diana's last official photo shoot with Mario Testino in May 1997.

In the late 1980s Diana favoured simpler styles and particular favourites were Catherine Walker's coat dresses. This red dress with white edging was worn with a matching hat designed by Philip Somerville at a passing-out parade at the Royal Naval College in Dartmouth in April 1989.

romantic creations by the Emanuels, Gina Fratini, Bellville Sassoon and Catherine Walker. These were usually made of floating fabrics, such as chiffon, in light colours with small patterns and often shot-through with metallic threads. However, the Princess also enjoyed wearing simpler gowns, such as the Hachi dress, and both styles coexisted for another ten years. Diana wore a romantic, Russian ballet-inspired dress by the Emanuels on three occasions between 1986 and 1987, while only one year earlier she had chosen a very different, simple Bruce Oldfield dress in black velvet.

Diana's gradual move towards a simpler look was also reflected in mainstream fashion. The economic euphoria of the 1980s was followed by record unemployment and recession. The need for security in an ever-faster changing world was also expressed in fashion: the sharp, exaggerated designs of the eighties were superseded by softer styles made of draping materials in rich colours. The motto 'less is more' was applied to the female wardrobe that was now focused on basics: classically cut blazers and trouser suits, slim skirts and polo necks.

From the late 1980s onwards Diana bought the majority of her wardrobe from fewer designers and her style became more unified. Catherine Walker, who together with Victor Edelstein provided most of her evening dresses and a large part of her daytime working wardrobe, was in no small way responsible for this style change. When Diana was mentioned on the International Best Dressed List in

1991/2 she was praised in equal terms for 'having established an appropriate, non-dowdy modern style of royal dress and bringing world recognition to young British designers'.

In December 1993, Diana announced that she would withdraw from most of her public duties. She now spent much of her free time on treatments for her body and soul and was often photographed in bicycle shorts and sweatshirts on her way to and from the gym. This led to unfavourable press reports describing her as a lady who lunched, shopped and toned her body but did very little else. While this might have been true for a short period, in the second half of 1994, without making a formal announcement, Diana again began to take on an increasing number of public engagements.

Previously Diana's private clothes had been very different from those for her public engagements, but both styles now merged. Her signature look for day was simple, unadorned suits in bright, camera-friendly colours with short narrow skirts that emphasized her long legs. Contrary to what many people believed, Diana had been wearing styles from international designers in private and also to select public appearances for some time. After the official separation from Prince Charles in December 1992, she could wear more openly her outfits by non-British fashion houses such as Chanel, Valentino, Moschino, Armani, Versace and Yves Saint Laurent. She also added new British designers to her stable such as Jacques Azagury, Tomasz Starzewski and Amanda Wakeley.

Diana no longer had to conform to the royal dress code and wore increasingly body-conscious styles that made the most of her well-toned shoulders and arms. Simple but effective shift dresses, often by Gianni Versace whose clothes Diana had worn in private since 1991, became the mainstay of her summer wardrobe. She now had fewer occasions to wear long evening gowns, but when she did so she preferred long versions of the shift dress style by Versace, Azagury and Catherine Walker. Gone were the flat shoes (worn to appear shorter than Prince Charles); Diana now strode out on high heels by Manolo Blahnik or Jimmy Choo. Her short, simple hairstyle by Sam McKnight and softer make-up fitted this new look perfectly.

Diana's early style may have had a greater influence on women's wardrobes, but what most people recall are the elegant suits and glamorous shift dresses of the 1990s. After 15 years of experimenting, Diana had found a style that suited her. Clothes that were less an expression of her role but that supported the modern, confident woman she had become.

Diana looking her most glamorous in New York in 1995. She is wearing a low-cut black dress with embroidered bodice by Jacques Azagury. Her shorter, slightly tousled hair matches the simplicity of the dress perfectly.

Diana – fashion icon?

Diana, Princess of Wales has often been called a 'fashion icon' and has been credited with almost single-handedly reviving the British fashion industry. Countless still and moving images recorded the Princess's sartorial development, which influenced and reflected the fashion changes of her contemporaries. Many commentators on Diana's wardrobe today focus on her later fashions, but it was the early 'Lady Di' style that was most widely imitated. When pictures of Diana were first published in the papers they were soon followed by articles analysing her style and in 1983 alone three books on the Princess's fashions were published. Susan Maxwell, who brought out an illustrated biography of the Princess of Wales as early as 1982, declared: 'For the first time, the Royal Family had in their ranks a woman whose age, size, coiffure and taste reflected the mass of the market. Because she was beautiful, others wanted to look like her'.

Diana's early admirers and enterprising retailers focused on fashion features that were easy to replicate. In an article in *Time* magazine in August 1981, it was reported that Lady Diana was 'already widely imitated – the hair, the clothes, the ruffled collars – but never duplicated' and Jane Owen remembered two years later that 'Lady Di' blouses 'run up by the mass market were selling like hot cakes'. The British department store Marks & Spencer sold many of these replicas and brought out their own Diana fashion book in 1984. Lyn Morris, Senior Selector for Marks & Spencer ladies' blouses, recalled: 'As soon as Diana did that engagement picture, our fastest selling style was a side-tying Diana blouse' sold at £9.99.

Rather unconvincing Diana lookalikes arrive at the headquarters of the Tory party in London in May 1997. While Diana's hemline had been creeping upwards during the 1990s, it was rarely as short as worn here.

For her first public appearance after the royal engagement was announced, Diana chose a black taffeta off-the-shoulder ballgown from the Emanuels. It was criticized for being too revealing, but the British tabloids loved it.

Mass-market fashion houses became ever more adept at producing replica styles in the shortest possible time and were well prepared for the royal wedding day. Although Diana's dress had remained a secret until the bride stepped out of the glass coach in front of St Paul's Cathedral, in the afternoon of the same day a similar dress made by Ellis Bridals went on sale at Debenhams department store for £439. Ronald Phillips of the company Ronald Joyce was planning to sell their own imitation for £290 and proudly told the papers that they 'started at 10.30 and finished at 2.30. We had six people working on it'. Another company, Leshgold, offered an even cheaper version made of paper taffeta for only £275 with an optional extra headdress and tiara for £10. Susan Matys, a beauty consultant from Harrow, was one of the first to try on the Ellis Bridals dress but decided to consult her fiancé before making a final decision. It was reported that Debenhams even presented a delighted Beverley Saunders '17 years old and very much in love' with a free copy of the dress as 'a gesture of faith in the Royal Wedding'.

Even dresses that were criticized sparked off imitations. *The New Standard* reported that Diana's appearance in the infamous black taffeta Emanuel dress resulted in the rag trade 'happily running up miles of black flounces … what she did for black taffeta, Lady Diana can do for pierrot collars and Peruvian knitwear, sailor suits, polka dots and pearls. Everyone can cash in – and they do'. In 1982 a Tailors and Garment Workers Union official declared:

'Princess Di has been a gift from the gods when our industry was dying' and noted that 'every factory I walk around is producing Princess Di clothes'.

Diana's layered haircut with the carefully blow-dried fringe was also widely copied, and not only in Britain. When Prince Charles toured New Zealand and Australia soon after the engagement, he was confronted by five Diana lookalikes who all had their hair styled the same way. Those who were hesitant to cut their hair could buy a Diana wig and wear it with an imitation engagement ring, a snip at only £8. Richard Dalton, a stylist at Kevin Shanley's salon Head Lines, took over from Shanley in late 1984 and was responsible for Diana's short-lived longer hairstyle after the birth of Prince Harry. When Diana appeared with her hair swept back off her face in forties style the story stayed in the press for days. As Diana's hair was 'such a major thing', Dalton and the Princess decided to make subsequent changes in a more subtle way: 'If we were going to change her style, like when we were going to Saudi Arabia where we decided her hair would probably be more suitable short, we'd do it over a period of weeks, so it would be every other day, snip, snip, snip, so you didn't notice it'.

It was not only the cheaper end of the market that profited from the Diana fashion phenomenon. The designer Caroline Charles, who provided many of Diana's early outfits, remembered that 'a lot of international press and buyers came to London in the Eighties because of her, just as

Aware of the strict dress code for women in Saudi Arabia, Diana chose a long tunic and trousers by Catherine Walker to wear to a desert picnic in Riyadh in November 1986. The press reported that her crescent-shaped earrings were a present from her host but they came from the Princess's own collection of costume jewellery.

The large red polka dots on Diana's dress echo the rising sun motif on Japan's national flag. The dress was worn on the first day of a royal tour of Japan in 1986. It was purchased by Diana from Tatters, a small shop in London's Fulham Road.

they'd come in the Sixties because of the Beatles'. The designer David Sassoon commented in 1989 that Diana 'has the best image we could possibly hope to have for this country. We are very lucky to have someone as glamorous and as pretty as she is. For us she is a miracle worker'.

Royal tours abroad were an effective showcase for British fashion. In 1986 the Prince and Princess of Wales went on a four-week tour of Canada and Japan. Long before the couple arrived in Japan 'Di Mania' had reached fever pitch. Women's magazines were full of features on the Princess's style and photographs of her even appeared on Tokyo phonecards. In one department store a Princess Diana lookalike competition was held, where young Japanese girls paraded in ruffle-necked blouses and pearls. Diana was careful to include appropriate cultural symbols into her wardrobe as a compliment to the country she was visiting. When she attended a traditional tea ceremony on her first day in Japan, the Princess wore a white dress with large red polka dots with a red straw hat by Frederick Fox that repeated the 'rising sun' motif. To a banquet with Emperor Hirohito on the last evening of the tour, Diana wore a Fortuny-inspired pleated blue silk dress by Yuki, a Japanese designer working in London.

Diana's official clothes were closely scrutinized but did not relate closely to the fashions of her contemporaries.

Off-duty, for instance when watching Prince Charles playing polo or taking her sons to school, Diana wore clothes that could have come out of the wardrobes of her many fans and were more affordable and more easily imitated than her state gowns. Diana's patterned knitted sweaters in particular started, or more likely accelerated, a trend. For an official photo shoot with the Prince at Balmoral in May 1981, Diana wore a Peruvian knitted jumper over Margaret Howell corduroy trousers tucked into green wellington boots. Once the source of the sweater, a local shop called 'Inca', was revealed in the papers, 500 of the same design were sold within three days. The shop owners told the Press: 'People would ring up and say "Can I have the Lady Di sweater", or fudge the issue and ask for the sweater with lamas and rows of girls on it'.

When Diana was pictured in her famous black sheep jumper, a present from a friend from 'Warm and Wonderful', it had a similar effect. Johanna Osborne, one of the two owners of the shop, told the author of the *Royal Shopping Guide* in 1984 'it really helped our business … in fact it is still selling, although the Princess wore it before she got married. We are trying hard to do other things, but we can't get away from the sheep sweater'. Even David Bowie was said to have bought a version in different colours.

While certain items of Diana's casual wardrobe had an effect on the High Street, the influence also worked the

In the early 1980s Diana wore a number of colourful sweaters that were widely copied. The Peruvian jumper worn at a photo shoot at Balmoral Castle in May 1981 (above) was particularly popular – as was the black-sheep jumper worn by the Princess on several occasions including here at a polo match in June 1983.

Diana with Prince William at a polo match in Windsor in 1988. She is wearing a sweatshirt with the logo of the British Lung Foundation, a charity the Princess supported. Oversized men's jackets were very popular in the late 1980s.

other way. Dungarees, large men's shirts, espadrilles and moccasins were not only worn by Diana, but by teenagers and twenty-somethings all over Europe. The same could be said of jeans, cowboy boots and T-shirts or sweatshirts bearing logos. There was a small difference: Diana had worn denim all her life, but her jeans were no longer from Fiorucci, Benetton or Jean Machine, but from Margaret Howell, Rifat Ozbek and later Armani and Versace. Her T-shirts did not display the logos of her favourite bands, but those of the charities she was a patron of. In the early 1990s photographs of Diana on her way to and from the gym often appeared in the press. While not every woman would have wanted to emphasize the shape of her legs by wearing tight-fitting bicycle shorts, it wasn't Diana's outfit that was unusual, but the fact that no one had ever seen a picture of a member of the royal family in casual sporting gear.

Diana's early fashions were more idiosyncratic than her later styles and her choices were criticized by some fashion commentators. In 1981 the Princess of Wales even topped the notorious '10 Worst Dressed List' compiled since 1960 by the one-time fashion designer Richard Blackwell. But Diana's early style was unique and very much her own and even her formal outfits included elements that could be replicated and fitted into the wardrobe of someone leading a very different life from that of the Princess. Her simpler and fashionable later style, however, was much more difficult to copy for the mass market as it depended on high-quality fabrics and perfect cuts. In the 1990s,

Diana's fashions were still closely examined, but fewer people could hope to buy a piece of the Diana magic.

Certain elements of the Princess's wardrobe continued to have the power to start a worldwide trend. In September 1995, Diana received a 'Lady Dior' handbag – often wrongly assumed to have been named after the Princess – from Bernadette Chirac, the wife of the French President. Diana was frequently photographed with different versions of the bag and it sold out all over Europe with a worldwide waiting list. In the early 1980s, a large part of the female population could afford a Diana replica blouse from Marks & Spencer but the Lady Dior bag at several hundred pounds was out of the reach of most of her admirers.

The Princess had her own favourite styles that never made it into the general fashion vocabulary. Asymmetric dresses had briefly been fashionable in the 1980s, but continued to be worn by the Princess throughout her life.

'I wasn't mad on one-sleeve dresses but she loved them and, by then, I'd learned that she couldn't be convinced on certain things, so I popped a beaded white one-sleeve Hachi dress on the rail and trotted over to Kensington Palace. Sure enough she made a beeline for it, and when I saw the newspaper pictures of her wearing it, I realized her instincts had been right.'

Anna Harvey

Diana loved asymmetric dresses and continued to wear them long after they ceased to be fashionable. This white silk crêpe dress embroidered with flat sequins and bugle beads by Catherine Walker was designed for a state visit to Brazil in April 1991. Diana wore it again to a film premiere in September of the same year.

*Diana commissioned several
designs with a nautical theme
from Catherine Walker including
this navy silk dress with gold
braid from 1990.*

*This tailcoat-shaped jacket worn
over a bustier dress by Catherine
Walker (above) perfectly
combines Diana's love of
masculine styles with a very
feminine shape. It was worn to a
film premiere in February 1990.*

Nautical or military inspired outfits were another favourite of Diana's in the 1980s. Until the mid-1980s the Princess wore a number of 'Cossack'-style coats and hats that sparked off a minor trend. Less successful was a Catherine Walker design worn twice in 1987. The white suit with gold frogging and epaulettes, worn with a hat by Graham Smith at Kangol, was likened to a 'drum majorette' outfit and was said by some to make Diana look like a member of Sergeant Pepper's Lonely Hearts Club Band.

In the late 1980s Diana was often seen in men's suits, another style she adopted from the High Street but continued to wear long after its popularity had reached its peak. When Yves Saint Laurent had included a smoking jacket in his haute couture collection for 1966, it was seen as a symbol of female emancipation. While not many could afford the original, tuxedos and men's jackets could be found in the second-hand shops that proliferated in the late 1960s and 1970s. At first this style was reserved for members of subcultures such as punk and the underground music scene. When Diane Keaton was filmed in chinos, a man's shirt, tie and waistcoat for Woody Allen's film *Annie Hall* in 1977, it alerted the High Street to the feminine potential of the male wardrobe. In the mid-1980s the androgynous style was again popularized by Annie Lennox, the singer of Eurythmics.

At a Genesis charity concert in February 1984 Diana was photographed chatting with members of the band in a tuxedo dinner suit by Margaret Howell, complete with black bow tie. During a visit to Italy in April 1985 the Princess wore a green skirt suit by Jasper Conran with a white shirt and matching green tie. Two years later, attending the ballet in Portugal, she chose another Jasper Conran outfit: a voluminous black satin bustle skirt with a bright orange jacket worn with a black bow tie instead of jewellery. Like the asymmetrical dresses, this was a style Diana adhered to until the 1990s. In 1994 she visited her nephew in hospital in a masculine suit by Escada adorned with golden elephants at the cuff and on the matching belt. Diana wore the suit with a white shirt, a black tie with white polka dots and her favourite, slightly tattered, brown suede Chelsea boots.

While Diana's more idiosyncratic forays into fashion were not copied widely, many women saw, and continue to see, her, as their sartorial role model. Diana herself was not immune to imitation and chose her own fashion icons carefully. According to Georgina Howell 'for inspiration towards finding her own identity in fashion … the Princess was more interested in movie stars: constantly photographed beauties whose personalities were more important than their clothes'.

Marilyn Monroe, Grace Kelly and Audrey Hepburn had been equally famous as the Princess. While Diana could give a good impression of walking like Monroe in *Some Like it Hot* for private consumption, she more publicly embraced the style of Grace Kelly, whom she had first met in 1981.

Diana's mess jacket (far left) was provided by the gentlemen's tailors Gieves and Hawkes and was worn to a dinner of the Royal Hampshire Regiment in Winchester in February 1990.

Not everyone liked Diana's drum majorette outfit by Catherine Walker, worn at Sandhurst Military Academy in April 1987.

Diana in one of her 'Jackie Kennedy' suits by Versace during a visit to the 2nd Battalion of the Queen's and Royal Hampshire Regiment in Canterbury in May 1995. Philip Somerville provided the matching pillbox hat. Diana wore the suit again in November of the same year during a trip to Argentina.

Included in the Christie's auction of Diana's dresses was an ice-blue chiffon dress and stole by Catherine Walker, inspired by a similar dress worn by Grace Kelly in Alfred Hitchcock's *To Catch a Thief*. Photographs of Audrey Hepburn from the late 1950s might also have been the inspiration for the black outfit Diana wore at a sitting with the photographer Patrick Demarchelier in 1991.

The most important of Diana's role models was Jackie Kennedy. Both women have been called the greatest single fashion influence in modern history, but there were more fundamental similarities. Like Jackie, Diana had married into a powerful family and, like the Wales's, the Kennedy wedding went down in history. Both women had eclipsed their husbands on foreign visits and both had been famously photographed alone in front of the Taj Mahal. The Princess studied Jackie's wardrobe and, at a charity dinner in Washington in 1985, spent a large part of the evening questioning her neighbour about her. In 1995 Diana wore a pink, fitted suit by Versace, similar to Jackie Kennedy's famous Chanel suit. In 1997 the Princess chose a similar Versace suit in pale blue for Prince William's confirmation. According to Philip Somerville, who provided the pillbox hats for both occasions, 'Diana adored pillboxes. And she liked to wear them as Jackie Kennedy did, on the back of the head to show her thick fringe.' Somerville did not reveal how he answered the question Diana once asked him: 'Do you think one day, people will think of me as the Jackie Kennedy of my day?'

Photographing Diana

The Princess of Wales was probably the most photographed woman of the 20th century. Before Diana, only Marilyn Monroe, Jackie Kennedy and Grace Kelly at the time of her wedding attracted a similar level of media attention. When Diana became a member of the royal family, she could expect to be painted and photographed for official portraits and at public engagements. While she could exert a certain amount of control over commissioned images, she could not control the thousands of snapshots the paparazzi would take of her. Both types of representation were instrumental in shaping her image.

Until the invention of photography in the late 1830s, painted state portraits and sculpture were the main methods available to reproduce a monarch's likeness. In 1842, Prince Albert, the Prince Consort, was the first member of a royal family to appear on a daguerrotype, the earliest permanent photographic process. After 1857 and the introduction of the 'carte-de-visite', a paper print mounted on to a small card board, photography soon marginalized older forms of mass-produced imagery and was used by royal families all over Europe as a publicity tool. While photographs could not be reproduced directly in the press until the beginning of the 20th century, illustrations based on photographs began to appear in newspapers and magazines from the late 1840s.

This new type of portrait proliferated at a time when the powers of monarchy all over Europe were increasingly curtailed. Members of the royal family are photographed

Diana sitting slightly uncomfortably, it seems, on an 18th-century throne that is usually on display in the State Apartments at Kensington Palace. Lord Snowdon took this official photograph in 1991. The deep aubergine silk velvet dress by Victor Edelstein was sold in the 1997 Christie's auction.

Lord Lichfield was the official photographer at Charles and Diana's wedding in 1981. As well as the customary formal photographs of the royal couple, he also managed to obtain some less traditional shots.

Cecil Beaton's photograph of Queen Elizabeth was taken shortly after her coronation in 1953, in the Green Drawing Room at Buckingham Palace. The Queen is shown in full regalia in front of an artificial background depicting St George's Chapel, Windsor. In this image, Beaton successfully evokes traditional state portraits.

almost from the day they are born and a succession of images marking important life or national events ensures that the general public can follow their lives closely. Queen Victoria started this practice and sat for the camera on numerous occasions, becoming the most photographed woman of her age. Right from the start, two types of royal photography emerged: the informal, encouraged by Prince Albert, and the more formal and staged arrangements preferred by the Queen.

The mixture of formal state portraits and photographs simulating family snapshots has continued to this day. In the former, the sitter is shown immobile, standing or seated, wearing evening dress or uniform, in front of an artificial or blurred studio background or in one of the royal residences. These photographs emphasize tradition, wealth and power and highlight the fact that the royal person is different from us. Cecil Beaton's photographs of the newly anointed Queen Elizabeth II in full regalia for the coronation of 1953 are a good example of this style. Informal portraits show the sitter in casual, often country, dress, sharing a private moment, and prove that the royal family is 'just like us'. It is the combination of both types of photography that is so powerful, inspiring awe and empathy at the same time.

Particular photographers were chosen to aid a particular message. Beaton's romantic images of Queen Elizabeth, later The Queen Mother, in 1939 played an important role in the transformation of the down-to-earth Duchess of York into what Beaton himself called 'the fairy Queen in her ponderous Palace'. Beaton was used to photographing stars and fashion models and transported his royal sitter into a dreamlike, fairy-tale world, which remained the main model for official royal photography until the late 1960s. More importantly, after Beaton, photography became the main form of imagery through which the royal family was seen. Painting and sculpture were finally relegated to the margins.

Photography was the powerful medium that connected Diana with her adoring public. The mixture of formal and casual was also adhered to in the official photographs of Prince Charles and Lady Diana. Often two sets of photographs were taken at the same sitting, as was the case with the royal engagement photographs by Lord Snowdon. Snowdon had been taking photographs of the royal family since The Queen and the Duke of Edinburgh made their tour of Canada in 1957, and continued to do so after his divorce from Princess Margaret in 1978. The informal shots of Charles and Diana show them in matching light blue Oxford shirts. Diana, her sleeves rolled up, embraces Charles and prominently displays her engagement ring. The smiling couple are photographed in front of a neutral, sky-blue backdrop and Diana's ring is the only attribute that distinguishes the pair from any ordinary couple.

Another set of photographs by Lord Snowdon taken before the wedding conforms more readily to the convention of the state portrait. This time the Prince

Lord Snowdon took this photograph of Diana with Prince William to mark the royal couple's first wedding anniversary on 29 July 1982. Catherine Walker had been asked via Vogue *to supply a 'beige or cream or pale blue dress for a formal portrait of someone special'.*

is standing in his full dress uniform next to a seated Diana in an emerald green taffeta ball gown by Nettie Vogues, accessorized with a diamond necklace and matching drop earrings. The couple's status, already expressed in their clothes, is further emphasized by the background: a large tapestry showing a hunting scene.

Patrick Lichfield, who had first been commissioned to photograph The Queen in 1971, was appointed official photographer at Charles and Diana's wedding. Lichfield followed the tradition established at the wedding of Princess Mary, eldest daughter of George V, to Henry, Viscount Lascelles in 1922, when the royal couple were photographed against the impressive background of the Throne Room at Buckingham Palace. Although Lichfield was not given much time, he successfully managed to shoot the customary group portraits as well as the newly-weds on their own. He included a few less traditional shots: the Princess seated on the steps with her long train spread out around her, the Prince and Princess kissing and a photograph of the couple and their bridesmaids and pages falling about with laughter.

From then on, at least one official photograph of the royal couple was taken each year for their Christmas card, until 1993 when Charles and Diana started to send separate cards. Official photographs were also commissioned to mark events such as the birth of the two princes or special birthdays. Sometimes Diana's clothes were made especially,

'[Diana] enjoyed sitting for portraits ... She especially loved Terence Donovan, who made her laugh, and Patrick Demarchelier, who was incredibly flirtatious and not remotely deferential. Snowdon perhaps, understood better than anyone what was required.'

Anna Harvey, *Vogue*, October 1997

as in summer 1982 when Lord Snowdon took a series of photographs to mark the couple's first wedding anniversary. The Princess's simple dress was made by Catherine Walker, who remembered receiving a request via *Vogue* for a '"beige or cream or pale blue dress for a formal portrait of someone special". It was as vague as that and we could only assume it was for the Princess. Since we had her measurements we were able to make this oyster silk faconné dress which we saw on every front page a day later'.

While Lord Snowdon was the photographer of choice to commemorate important family events, official portraits of the Princess were commissioned from other photographers. Terence Donovan and David Bailey, who had captured, and in many ways helped create, the Swinging Sixties in London, both photographed the Princess in the second half of the 1980s. Donovan's images largely conform to the traditional style: the Princess is depicted seated, in long evening gowns, her hands resting in her lap with her engagement ring prominently displayed. David Bailey's more unusual photographs from 1988 were commissioned by the trustees of the National Portrait Gallery. The Princess's casual stance – leaning against a wall with her hands in her pockets – is supported by her informal clothes: white blouse, dark

Terence Donovan photographed the Princess for the last time in 1990. In a probably deliberate imitation of Cecil Beaton's 1939 photographs of The Queen Mother, Diana is shown wearing an elaborate white evening dress by Victor Edelstein, made for a state banquet at the Elysée Palace in Paris. At £55,000 this was the most expensive dress the Princess had ever bought.

This elaborately staged photograph by Lord Snowdon in 1991 was the last official image of Diana and Prince Charles together. Lord Snowdon had been photographing Diana since 1981 and was later to take the photographs for the Christie's sales catalogue of her dresses in 1997.

pinstripe trousers and a black patent leather belt. Her monochrome outfit mirrors the stark black and white background. Like the change in Diana's style in the late 1980s and early 1990s towards a more simplified look, Bailey's photographs foreshadow the more minimal style of portraits that would soon be taken by Patrick Demarchelier and, most famously, Mario Testino.

In 1991 Lord Snowdon took the last official photograph of Prince Charles, Diana and the two princes. This carefully contrived group portrait shows the Prince in a double-breasted city suit, while Diana and the boys are wearing riding clothes. The 'props' include half-opened hampers, cast-iron garden furniture and leather-covered flasks – not forgetting a pony. The photograph resembles a Ralph Lauren promotional shot while at the same time making reference to 18th-century conversation pieces like those by the painters Johann Zoffany and Thomas Gainsborough. It was well known that Diana, following a childhood accident, was terrified of riding. Nor did she usually pose with animals, although being depicted with horses, hounds (or corgis) is another royal and aristocratic tradition. It is almost as if this is a last attempt to force Diana, one year before the separation of the royal couple was officially announced, into a visual tradition that she was never really part of and would soon escape from completely. Others have argued that Lord Snowdon made a deliberate comment on a marriage that, by then, only survived on the public stage.

By the time this last family portrait was taken, ten years after the wedding, official photographs had become overshadowed by the increasing number of newspaper images taken during royal engagements and the illicit shots of the paparazzi. Diana's rise to international media stardom is very closely linked to changes in the objectives of newspaper and magazine publishers and in their attitude to the royal family.

Since the emergence of television in the 1950s and the Internet in the 1990s, newspaper readership has been on a steady decline. Since the 1970s, entertainment and gossip have become more and more important to sell magazines and newspapers. Celebrity magazines are nothing new, they appeared at the same time as the film industry for which they were, and are, an important publicity tool. The introduction of hand-held cameras in the 1920s led to the birth of a number of magazines devoted to photojournalism such as *Vu* and *Match* (later *Paris Match*) in France, *Picture Post* in the UK and *Life* and *Look* in the US. These magazines increasingly included stories on celebrities and royalty. The first royal victim of press intrusion was Princess Margaret. The glamorous Princess had long been a favourite of the illustrated magazines and had often graced the cover of *Picture Post*. When the Princess fell in love with a divorced man, Group Captain Peter Townsend, in 1953, details of their relationship began to appear in many British newspapers and photographers followed the couple everywhere.

The royal family was forced to aid this increasing intrusion into their private lives. Ever since the coronation of Queen Elizabeth had been televised live in 1953, every major royal event has appeared on television. In 1967, the Palace Press Officer, Commander Richard Colville, whose dislike of the media was well known, was succeeded by William Heseltine. Recognizing that the royal family was no longer the automatic focus of admiration and reverence as in the past, Heseltine, who was supported by the Duke of Edinburgh, realized the importance of television in selling the royal family to the public. The immediate result was the commissioning of the BBC film *Royal Family*, which allowed cameras to record the daily life of The Queen and her family for the first time. The programme was watched by 68 per cent of the British population when it was aired in June 1969.

In the 1970s a number of magazines were launched to focus on 'extraordinary people doing ordinary things and ordinary people doing extraordinary things', the formula described by an editor of the US magazine *People*, first published in 1974. Celebrity news often made the front page of the tabloids and also invaded the broadsheets. The pre-war media

Patrick Demarchelier's most famous portraits of Diana were taken in 1991 for an issue of Vogue *magazine celebrating the English National Ballet, of which Diana was a patron. The Princess, with a new short haircut by Sam McKnight, is wearing a simple black polo neck.*

While Diana did not seem to mind being photographed at public events, the complete invasion of her privacy sometimes became too much for her. One paparazzo photographed Diana running away from another in June 1994.

had been deferential to the royal family and no stories had appeared in the domestic press about the affair between Edward, Prince of Wales and the twice-divorced Wallis Simpson, although it was widely commented upon in foreign newspapers. But during the 1980s the tone of royal reporting was to change forever.

Diana had been hunted by the media ever since her relationship with Prince Charles had become public and after her divorce the Princess was photographed by the paparazzi wherever she went. Magazine and newspaper editors knew that their circulation could increase by as much as 30 or 40 per cent by putting Diana on the cover and even the more reputable newspapers and magazines were not immune to this effect.

The death of Diana set a new media record. It was later estimated that one third of the pages published by British newspapers at this time was coverage of Diana. Most newspapers were selling 25 to 50 per cent above their normal circulation during the week from Diana's death to the funeral. *Hello* magazine doubled its circulation and Diana's images continue

to be devoured by members of the public despite the worldwide condemnation of the paparazzi after the Princess's death.

However much Diana might have hated the press intrusion into her private life, she was also very aware that photographs of her at charity events could greatly boost awareness of their causes. A picture of Diana shaking hands with an AIDS patient was worth a hundred articles, and her presence generated millions of pounds in donations to her charities. While the tabloids were most ferocious in the intrusion, they were also often far more supportive of her charity work than the broadsheets.

Photographs of the Princess were not only taken at high-profile events but also depicted her doing things many women of a similar age could relate to: taking the children to school, going to the gym, shopping and having a night out with friends. These images brought Diana closer to her admiring public and meant that many people thought they knew who she really was. They empathized with her, compared themselves to her and some even thought that the Princess was their own personal friend.

These unofficial photographs at the same time emphasized the fact that Diana belonged to a different world. Not many people can be snapped from a difficult angle, without studio lighting, and still look glamorous. However, some of the paparazzi photographs were taken not to inspire reverence, but to humiliate. Diana is the first royal person who was consistently treated as a 'celebrity', both irrespective of her role as a member of the royal family and because of it.

Commissioned royal photographs once differed dramatically from unofficial images, but the division became increasingly blurred and the particular quality of the paparazzi photographs, emphasizing movement and spontaneity, started to influence commissioned portraits of the Princess. The French-born Patrick Demarchelier, who became the first non-British photographer to officially photograph a member of the royal family, noted that Diana 'was very good in front of the camera, very natural, but at the same time you had to talk to her or she could freeze very easily. The best thing was to take her off her guard. That's why the paparazzi pictures are all so fantastic. I had to recreate that, to make her relaxed, happy, laughing'.

Photographic historian Martin Harrison has described Demarchelier's images as 'unforced and convincingly spontaneous' and it was probably these qualities that led Diana to commission Demarchelier to photograph her and the princes in 1990. As Harrison noted, in many of his portraits Demarchelier 'focuses on the head and crops

The flashlights of the paparazzi
cameras falling on Diana as she
arrived at an evening event,
often gave her a special aura.
This spangled mermaid dress
by Catherine Walker (left) worn
in 1986 and again in 1990
enhances this effect by reflecting
the light.

Diana strides confidently along
a red carpet at a charity dinner
dance in Sydney, Australia, in
October 1996. In her deceptively
simple turquoise silk dress by
Versace and matching T-bar
shoes she looks like a supermodel
on a catwalk.

Diana looking radiant during her last official photo shoot with Mario Testino in May 1997. Testino remembered that Diana 'was really divine that day. She looked so happy and fresh and sure of herself'.

tightly around the shoulder line, bringing the hands into the frame as an expressive element which he uses to great effect'. Elaborate clothing spoils this effect and Diana and her sons were depicted in jeans and simple, light shirts that do not detract from their faces.

Demarchelier's most famous portrait of Diana was taken in 1991 for an issue of *Vogue* magazine celebrating the English National Ballet, of which Diana was a patron. The Princess, with a new short haircut, is wearing a very simple black polo neck and trousers, reminiscent of Audrey Hepburn's beatnik clothes in the 1957 Hollywood film *Funny Face*. In 1992, the year of the separation, Demarchelier photographed Diana in a stunning Versace dress with her hair gelled back, sitting in front of a plain white background. The photograph is hardly distinguishable from a fashion shoot but, in an amusing aside, the Princess's status has crept into the picture: she is sitting on a pedestal.

In March 1997 probably the most well-known portraits of the Princess were taken to promote the Christie's dress auction. To complement Lord Snowdon's more formal photographs, Meredith Etherington-Smith suggested that the fashion and portrait photographer Mario Testino should photograph Diana for the magazine *Vanity Fair*. Several features contribute to the immediacy of Testino's photographs. No tiara, no diamond-encrusted necklace, no earrings or bracelets denote Diana's status. No immaculate coiffure, but a haircut that is at the same time classic and modern and moves with the sitter. What is most striking are the Princess's poses, or rather that she does not pose at all. The most engaging photographs show her laughing, seemingly sharing a joke with the photographer, moving around not on high heels, but barefoot. Even when the Princess is sitting on the simple white sofa specially commissioned for the shoot (no red velvet or gilded wood here), she seems not to be in a photographer's studio but at home. The images look like the kind of photographs you would take of a friend, trying on various outfits for a night out.

The nine dresses worn for the Testino shoot are very simple, slimline (with the exception of one ball gown) and made of tactile fabrics such as velvet. They seem to be the more personal, private dresses of the Princess, the ones she felt comfortable in, rather than the ones she bought to convey an official message.

Looking closely at photographs of Diana, we do not just observe the development of a shy kindergarten teacher, albeit with an aristocratic background, via Princess, to a confident, modern woman, for whom special royal paraphernalia have become obsolete. The photographs also reflect the increasing importance of images in our culture, our obsession with the lives of the famous and how images are used by those who commission them and those who publish them to determine how we judge a person we have never met. Looking at Diana's photographs, we might also learn something about ourselves.

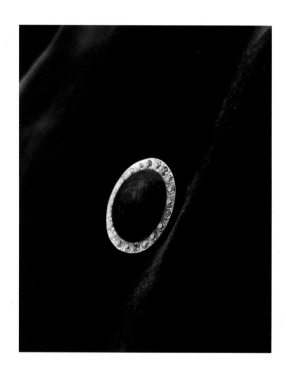

Catherine Walker made this dark-green silk velvet dress for Diana in 1992. Diana did not wear the dress in public but chose it as one of the nine dresses for the photo shoot with Mario Testino in May 1997.

Diana and her designers

In 1981 dress designers up and down the country would
have been delighted at the prospect of working for the
young, beautiful and vivacious Diana. Designing for a royal
client is both a pleasure and a challenge for any couturier.
There is the thrill of seeing one's work showcased and
brought to the widest possible audience, but at the same
time the designer will be aware that the dress of a person
regularly in the public eye has a job to do. Their design
independence may be circumscribed by the client who may
have a particular image they need to promote.

The immensely skilled tailors and dressmakers of earlier
generations are sadly unidentifiable and the role of the
couturier only begins to emerge in the later 19th century.
One of the first was the energetic and highly talented
Charles Frederick Worth. Born in humble circumstance in
Lincolnshire, Worth arrived in Paris in the 1840s and set up
a dressmaking service within the celebrated mercers' store,
Gagelin. This achieved such success that by 1857 he had
established his own company and soon captured the
custom of the Empress Eugenie and her ladies.

Queen Alexandra (consort of Edward VII) did not patronize
Worth, whose designs were considered too French for the
Queen of England. Instead, she favoured Redfern, a tailoring
company originally based on the Isle of Wight and the first
English fashion house to achieve an international reputation
for its design innovation. Queen Mary (consort of George V)
preferred the couturiers Reville and Rossiter, who supplied

Diana and Catherine Walker in Diana's drawing room at Kensington Palace in May 1987. They discuss Catherine's coat-dress of Riechers lace made for a state visit to France in 1988.

Queen Elizabeth was photographed by Cecil Beaton in the garden of Buckingham Palace in July 1939. She wears a dress by Norman Hartnell of silk chiffon trimmed with lace and embroidered with beads. This was a style of dress he devised for her in 1938, and which proved so successful it became associated with the Queen for many years. The outfit is completed with an elegant parasol and a lace-trimmed hat, the wide brim swept up to reveal her face.

her coronation dress in 1911 and helped her develop a style that was both dated and timeless.

In the 1930s, it had been Norman Hartnell who helped create a powerful personal image for Queen Elizabeth The Queen Mother, which is recorded in the remarkable photographs of Cecil Beaton. His greatest achievement was the creation of her 'White Wardrobe' which she wore during a state visit to France, shortly after her husband's accession to the throne in 1937. Her mother died just before the visit and at the last minute Hartnell designed a 'white for mourning' wardrobe of romantic lacy crinoline-style dresses. These suited admirably the Queen's slightly old-fashioned prettiness. A personal style had been created which for evening dress, and for much of her daywear too, came to be identified with the Queen for the next fifty years.

Queen Elizabeth II has a less pronounced dress style than either her grandmother or her mother. This does not mean that she has not been concerned with her sartorial image. She has always bought British and has patronized some of the most skilled couturiers and milliners of her generation. Her clothes and accessories are made of the finest fabrics and showcase the skill of dressmakers, embroiderers and beaders. They are often brightly coloured, eye-catching and practical and are always beautifully made.

So, Diana had a number of role models she could choose to follow. Would she carve out for herself a very particular personal style, and stick with it? Would she pick from the best of British dress design those styles that would enable her to do her job best? Her choice of designer would be the key to her making her own fashion statement.

Diana had encountered the work of David and Elizabeth Emanuel during the Snowdon photo shoot for *Vogue* in 1981. The Emanuels had graduated together from the Royal College of Art in 1977. It was an ebullient time in fashion and their trademark ruffles quickly caught on. They established a showroom in Brook Street and began to receive commissions from Joan Collins, Shirley Bassey and Elizabeth Taylor. Despite adverse press reaction to their revealing black taffeta dress, Diana would return to them to design her wedding dress a short time later.

Diana had first visited the designers Bellville Sassoon as a shy teenager. Belinda Bellville and David Sassoon had made some of her mother's – Frances Shand Kydd – favourite outfits and were delighted when Diana asked them to design the dress she would wear as she left for her honeymoon in July 1981. As her confidence grew David Sassoon recalls how pleased they were when the sketches they sent her arrived back with the pencilled message 'Yes please'. Even after Belinda Bellville retired from the company and was replaced by the designer Lorcan Mullany, the Princess continued her patronage into the 1990s.

David and Elizabeth Emanuel
in their studio in Brook Street,
London. They were the first
husband and wife team to study
fashion together at the Royal
College of Art.

Diana chose a pretty blue-and-
white dress by Bellville Sassoon
to wear at the opening of the
Gonzaga exhibition at the
Victoria and Albert Museum in
1982. The Princess, who was
pregnant at the time, fell asleep
during the speeches.

Wearing Victor Edelstein's Edwardian-style dark blue velvet evening dress, Diana took to the dance floor at the White House in 1985 with John Travolta. They danced to the song 'You're the one that I want'.

When in 1997, following her divorce, Diana made the decision to auction some of the dresses she would never wear again, the one that achieved the highest price was a dark blue velvet dress in an Edwardian style made by Victor Edelstein. It raised over £133,000 for the Princess's favourite charities. The dress was cut with a deep V neckline and the velvet ruched to follow the contours of her body, flaring out at the knee in a way that was perfect for dancing. And just as well! In 1985 the Prince and Princess of Wales were invited to the White House by President and Mrs Reagan. After dinner, dancing was suggested. The Princess had noticed that John Travolta was present and, to the delight of everyone there, she took a turn round the dance floor with him. The dress looked spectacular. 'That,' says Victor Edelstein 'is the mark of a good dress. It has to suit its purpose. When I design clothes I picture exactly how they will be seen and where – what kind of house, what kind of party – and I don't design for an abstract woman'.

Victor Edelstein started his career as a designer at Barbara Hulanicki's Biba in the 1960s. He enjoyed being part of the emerging youth culture and seeing his designs compared to those of his contemporaries: Mary Quant, Jean Muir, Sally Tuffin and Marion Foale, Kiki Byrne and John Bates. 'The clothes were young, I was young', he said. After moving to Christian Dior in the 1970s, where he worked on their 'ready-to-wear' collections, in 1982 he set up his own business to concentrate on doing what he liked best – making beautiful couture clothes. In this he achieved

great success. As well as the blue velvet evening dress
he made for the Princess there would be many others,
including the bold turquoise and black suit that she wore
to the wedding of the Duke and Duchess of York in 1986.

Zandra Rhodes, known to many for her trademark shocking-
pink hair, was a designer patronized by the Princess in the
early years of her marriage. In 1964 Zandra graduated from
the Royal College of Art where she studied textile design.
Her early work, which shows the influence of the pop
artists Andy Warhol and Roy Lichtenstein, was bold and
innovative. Encouragement from her colleague, the designer
Sylvia Ayton, while Zandra was teaching at Ravensbourne
College of Art led to the decision to use these textiles to
create her very first dresses, which were quickly snapped
up by Fortnum and Mason in London and Henri Bendal in
New York.

The textiles created by Zandra Rhodes remain the most
powerful element in her dress design, taking their inspiration
from the art and design traditions of India, China, Mexico,
Africa, Egypt and Greece. The rich patterns were
embellished still further with beading and embroidery. Mario
Testino would recall: 'When I came to London from Peru in
the 1970s, Zandra was all everyone was talking about in
fashion … her work was so unique … there are few
designers who have had that kind of ingenuity'. It was this
creativity that the Princess noticed. She visited Zandra's
shop in Grafton Street and tried on a number of dresses.

*A dress of white silk chiffon
embroidered with white and silver
beads by Zandra Rhodes. It was
worn by Diana in May 1987 to a
'Birthright' benefit at the London
Palladium. Proud of her work for
Princess Diana, Zandra Rhodes
assisted with the presentation of
the dress in an exhibition at
Kensington Palace.*

Diana and Bruce Oldfield attend a gala dinner at the Grosvenor House Hotel in November 1988. The dinner was in aid of the charity Dr Barnardo's. Diana wears a dress of luxurious purple crushed velvet that Bruce had designed for her the previous year for an official visit to Portugal.

Zandra recalled: 'I then went to Kensington Palace to personally fit her in one that had been made especially for her and in an exclusive print colour only for her'. The dress that the Princess had selected had a wrap skirt and deep V neckline. The delicate white on white print was highlighted with a scattering of white and silver beads. Zandra took great trouble with the commission: 'The dress as a wrap must not open too far or too awkwardly. The cross-over bust-line had to look sexy but never too low. She had to wear the dress, not the dress wear her!'

Bruce Oldfield was another designer whose work was sought out by the Princess. Not only did she enjoy his beautiful clothes, but she admired the way in which he had overcome so many challenges in his early life. Born in 1950, Bruce was brought up by the charity Dr Barnardo's. His foster mother, the extraordinary Violet Masters, a down-to-earth working class woman from County Durham, taught Bruce to knit and sew at an early age and encouraged his interest in art. As a teenager he moved back to a Dr Barnardo's home in North Yorkshire and was awarded a place at the local grammar school. He looked set for a career as a teacher, but during his time at Sheffield Teacher's College Bruce realized his real passion lay with fashion designing. In 1971 he negotiated a place at Ravensbourne College of Art, later transferring to St Martin's College of Art in London, where he studied dress design.

'Dressing her was quite different to dressing the divas who were going to swish parties. This was more a question of dressing a young woman who, to an extent, was relying on us to steer her straight ... She was a very good looking woman who knew where she was going but not necessarily in terms of style ... It was our job to give her that sophistication and help her develop her own style. She wanted the glamour that we could give her. And she got it.'

Bruce Oldfield

Bruce Oldfield designed dresses for the confident, modern woman. His power suits for the daytime were made to be worn with shoulder pads and high heels. For the evening his designs were glamorous and revealing to flatter a fit, well-toned body.

Bruce Oldfield's earliest work for Diana was undertaken through the auspices of Anna Harvey, the editor of *Vogue*. In 1981 he made her a 'very sharp rust Venetian suit' and a culotte suit, which she wore when turning on the Christmas lights in Bond Street. In 1982, he was asked to supply some maternity dresses. But it was not until 1985 when Diana's sartorial confidence had grown that he was asked to supply outfits on a more regular basis. Until the late 1980s, he created many daytime outfits and some of her most striking evening wear, including a smart black velvet dress with wide sweeping skirts worn at the opening of *Les Misérables* in November 1985, and the figure-hugging dress with a deep collar of purple crushed

velvet that she wore in Portugal on a state visit a few weeks later.

In 1985 Bruce Oldfield created one of the Princess's most glamorous outfits, which she wore at a charity gala and fashion show held at the Grosvenor House Hotel to raise money for Dr Barnardo's. It was made of a slinky pleated silver lamé, the fabric drawn up to cross over the bust and form straps over the deeply cut back. The Princess was president of the charity and it was entirely typical that she chose to wear such a striking dress designed by a Dr Barnardo's boy.

Undoubtedly the most enduring of Diana's designers was the elegant Frenchwoman Catherine Walker. Her entry into fashion was unorthodox. Born in 1945 she studied philosophy at the universities of Lille and Aix en Provence. Happily married to a successful English lawyer, the mother of two young children, her life was violently knocked off course

*Catherine Walker in her studio at
the Chelsea Design Company in
Sydney Street, London. Initially
Catherine specialized in making
clothes for children. In 1981, she
decided to concentrate on
women's wear and produced her
first collection of day, cocktail
and evening dresses.*

Catherine Walker incorporated into some of the outfits she designed for the Princess design details appropriate to the occasion where they were to be worn. This dress was designed for Diana to wear on a visit to India in 1992. The bodice and matching bolero are embroidered in a design reminiscent of the jewel-like Indian miniature paintings.

when her husband was killed in an accident. Making clothes for her daughters and later their friends and acquaintances started as a therapy in the early period of widowhood. As she taught herself pattern cutting, her skill and design sense became evident and her creations were snapped up by clients in fashionable west London. She had intended to walk from shop to shop selling the outfits from a wicker basket, but given how well her work was received she was encouraged by her new husband to set up her own business in Sydney Street. Her first venture into designing for adults was creating a line of maternity wear.

The first request Catherine Walker received from the Princess was again made via Anna Harvey and was for maternity dresses. One of the outfits supplied – a smocked dress of green spotted silk – was worn by the Princess as she left St Mary's Hospital, Paddington, with her husband and new son, Prince William. It was some months later before Catherine actually met the Princess. She visited Catherine's showroom to thank her for the dresses supplied earlier. Catherine sensed this was so she could 'take a discreet look at me and where I worked'.

For the next sixteen years Catherine Walker would supply hundreds of outfits to Diana including smart business suits and glamorous evening dresses. As Jasper Conran observed 'when she discovered Catherine Walker the Princess found what she needed – a designer who would design for her and concentrate on her'.

*This white silk crêpe dress by Catherine Walker was
worn by Diana for a state dinner held for the King
and Queen of Malaysia in 1992. It was one of the
dresses that Mario Testino chose to include in his
famous photo shoot with the Princess in 1997.*

Catherine was a skilled and selfless designer. She
recalls how she:

> developed a sense of how many different things
> the Princess had to be: a mother, a member of
> the royal family, the future Queen of England, an
> ambassador, an icon. She had all these roles to
> play, and, when asked, I as a designer was
> faced with the job of creating designs that would
> both reflect and enhance all of those roles ... My
> dream from the beginning had been to deal with
> Diana as a *real person* – to me it was as
> important as the designing.

Over the years, the empathy between Diana and
Catherine Walker became such that the designer
could predict the Princess's needs and provided
clothes which she knew Diana would enjoy wearing.

In 1992, for a visit to India and Pakistan, Catherine
provided the Princess with a dress of pink silk with a
bodice and matching bolero encrusted with colourful
embroidery inspired by traditional Indian miniature
painting. As Catherine noted, for these formal
moments her remit was to create 'a dignified
showstopper'. Arguably, the dress that surpassed

'My dream from the beginning had been to deal with Diana as a *real
person* – to me it was as important as the designing.'

Catherine Walker

Diana wore this elegant black dress by Catherine Walker at Versailles in 1994. It is trimmed with glossy black bugle beads around the neckline and at the waist. Catherine Walker took her inspiration for the beaded detail from a 17th-century picture frame.

them all was an elegant, black, slim-fitting halterneck, embroidered with glittering black bugle beads around the neckline. The dress was worn at a reception at the Palace of Versailles, arranged by UNESCO in December 1994 to celebrate the *Deuxième Nuit Internationale de l'Enfance*. Pierre Cardin commented 'This is the home of the sun king of France, now we have the sun princess of Versailles'.

As a fashion ambassador, Diana took her role seriously and while on official business would take care to wear outfits from a broad range of British designers. In the 1980s she commissioned outfits from young designers such as Arabella Pollen, Rifat Ozbek, Benny Ong, Alistair Blair and Jasper Conran, as well as more established names such as Roland Klein, Bill Pashley, Caroline Charles and Murray Arbeid. Donald Campbell made the pretty crêpe de Chine dress in which the Princess was photographed so memorably aboard the royal yacht during her honeymoon. Jan Vanvelden made some of her most successful maternity dresses with broad puritan collars, which Diana liked so much she had them adapted so she could continue to wear them as her children grew up. Gina Fratini, another graduate of the Royal College of Art, with a flare for romantic evening wear made of the lightest chiffons and silks, made a ball dress for the Princess to wear in New Zealand in 1983.

In the 1990s Diana enjoyed wearing clothes by Jacques Azagury, Tomasz Starzewski and Amanda Wakeley. The Princess had met Jacques Azagury at a London fashion show in 1985 but it was not until a few years later that she commissioned some of his simple and glamorous clothes for her wardrobe. He claims that he was responsible for shortening the length of the Princess's skirts: 'When I would pin up her hems, I would just try to go that little bit further'. Tomasz Starzewski specialized in 'lunch suits' and Amanda Wakeley in dresses with very clean lines made from the most luxurious fabrics.

Diana's outfits were set off with carefully chosen accessories. Hats were often an important part of the ensemble, although the Princess was concerned that her headwear should not add to her height. As a young woman Diana had rarely had the opportunity to wear them and at the time of her engagement she turned to her mother's favoured milliner John Boyd for her first commissions. He favoured small, head-hugging styles that were trimmed with a plume of feathers or a veil or a spray of flowers. This style suited the long, bobbed hairstyle that the Princess preferred at this time. Marina Kittery, a milliner introduced to Diana by Anna Harvey, was best known for making hats for fashionable wedding guests and encouraged the Princess to wear slightly larger styles. As Diana's

Philip Somerville designed a pagoda-shaped hat for Diana to wear during a state visit to Hong Kong in November 1989. It was later remade with a flat crown. The bright colours of the silk suit and crêpe T-shirt by Catherine Walker were chosen to echo the vibrant Chinese setting.

confidence grew she turned to Australian born Frederick Fox. He had begun to supply hats to The Queen in 1969 and had received his royal warrant in 1974. For Diana he made many large, brightly coloured hats with broad, up-sweeping brims to compliment her bolder dress choices.

Philip Somerville was another milliner favoured by Diana. The Princess had admired some of his work which she had spotted while watching television in 1986. Through her hairdresser Richard Dalton, she arranged an introduction. As well as making Diana's neat Jackie Kennedy pillbox hats which she wore perched on the back of her head, Somerville made the very pretty and clever headband with blue veil worn for the enthronement of the Emperor Akihito in Tokyo in 1990. The Princess also purchased hats from Stephen Jones and Graham Smith. Stephen Jones, who established his millinery business back in 1980, is known for the outrageous hats he made for Madonna, George Michael and Boy George. The Princess enjoyed the asymmetry of his styles. She also loved the pom-poms and other quirky details that are characteristic of Smith's work.

Shoes were another accessory which, while having to be practical and comfortable, if carefully chosen could help draw the whole outfit together. Manolo Blahnik still remembers Diana coming to visit on her bicycle as a teenager. Later she would arrive in a car with a driver and he would clear the shop of other customers before she made her purchases. Following her marriage Diana extended her business to Charles Jourdain, Ferragamo and Rayne, but sometimes still bought off-the-peg at Pied à Terre, Midas, Footloose and Hobbs.

As the Princess became more confident in her dress choices she came to appreciate the footwear made by Jimmy Choo, who made the majority of her shoes until her death in 1997. He made spectacular high heels, fabric covered, beaded and embroidered. But perhaps the Princess's favourite style of all was a low-heeled pump with a gently rounded toe, which could be made in any colour. They had a small V notch over the toe. Jimmy Choo still has the shoes in this style from the Princess's very last order, which he now treasures in her memory.

Index

Select bibliography

Ann Barr & Peter York, *The Official Sloane Ranger Handbook: The First Guide to What Really Matters in Life*, London: Ebury 1985

Alistair Burnett, *In Person: The Prince and Princess of Wales,* London: Michael O'Mara Books 1985

Diane Clehane, *Diana – the Secrets of Her Style*, New York: GT Publishing 1998

Rosalind Coward, *Diana: the Portrait*, London: Harper Collins Entertainment 2004

Colleen Denney, *Representing Diana, Princess of Wales: Cultural Memory and Fairy Tales Revisited*, Madison, NJ: Fairleigh Dickinson University Press 2005

Robin Derrick and Robin Muir (eds.), *People in Vogue: a Century of Portrait Photography*, London: Little, Brown 2003

Frances Dimond, *Developing the Picture: Queen Alexandra and the Art of Photography*: Royal Collection Publications 2004

Frances Dimond and Roger Taylor, *Crown & Camera: the Royal Family and Photography 1842–1910*, London: Viking 1987

David Emanuel and Elizabeth Emanuel, *A Dress for Diana*, London: Pavilion 2006

Jayne and Terry Fincher, *Debrett's Illustrated Fashion Guide: the Princess of Wales*, Exeter: Webb & Bower 1989

Tim Graham and Tamsin Blanchard, *Dressing Diana*, London: Weidenfeld & Nicholson 1998

Nina Grunfeld, *The Royal Shopping Guide*, London and Sydney: Pan Books 1984

Anna Harvey, 'Diana 1961–1997', *Vogue*, UK edition: October 1997

Georgina Howell, *Diana – Her Life in Fashion*, London: Pavilion Books 1998

Andrew Morton, *Diana's Diary: an Intimate Portrait of the Princess of Wales*, Michael London: O'Mara 1990

Bruce Oldfield with Fanny Blake, *Rootless*, London: Hutchinson 2004

Jane Owen, *Diana Princess of Wales: the Book of Fashion*, Guildford: Colour Library Books 1983

Ben Pimlott, *The Queen: Elizabeth II and the Monarchy*, London: Harper Collins 2001

Alexis Schwarzenbach, 'Royal Photographs: Emotions for the People', *Contemporary European History*, vol 13: Cambridge University Press 2004, pp. 255–280

Roy Strong, *Cecil Beaton: The Royal Portraits*, London: Thames and Hudson 1988

Catherine Walker, *Catherine Walker*, London: Harper Collins 1998